TO: ______________________

FROM: ______________________

AF538309

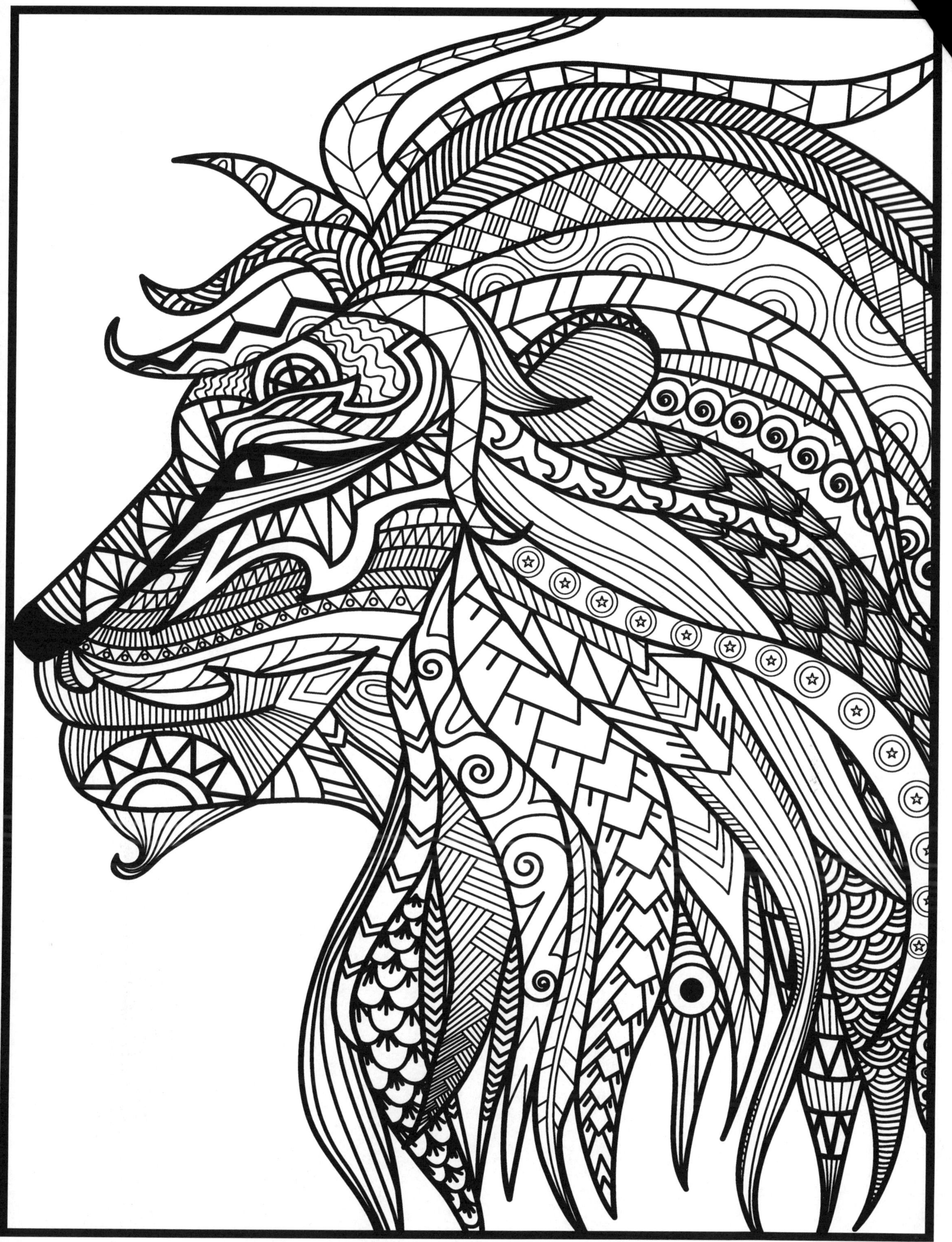

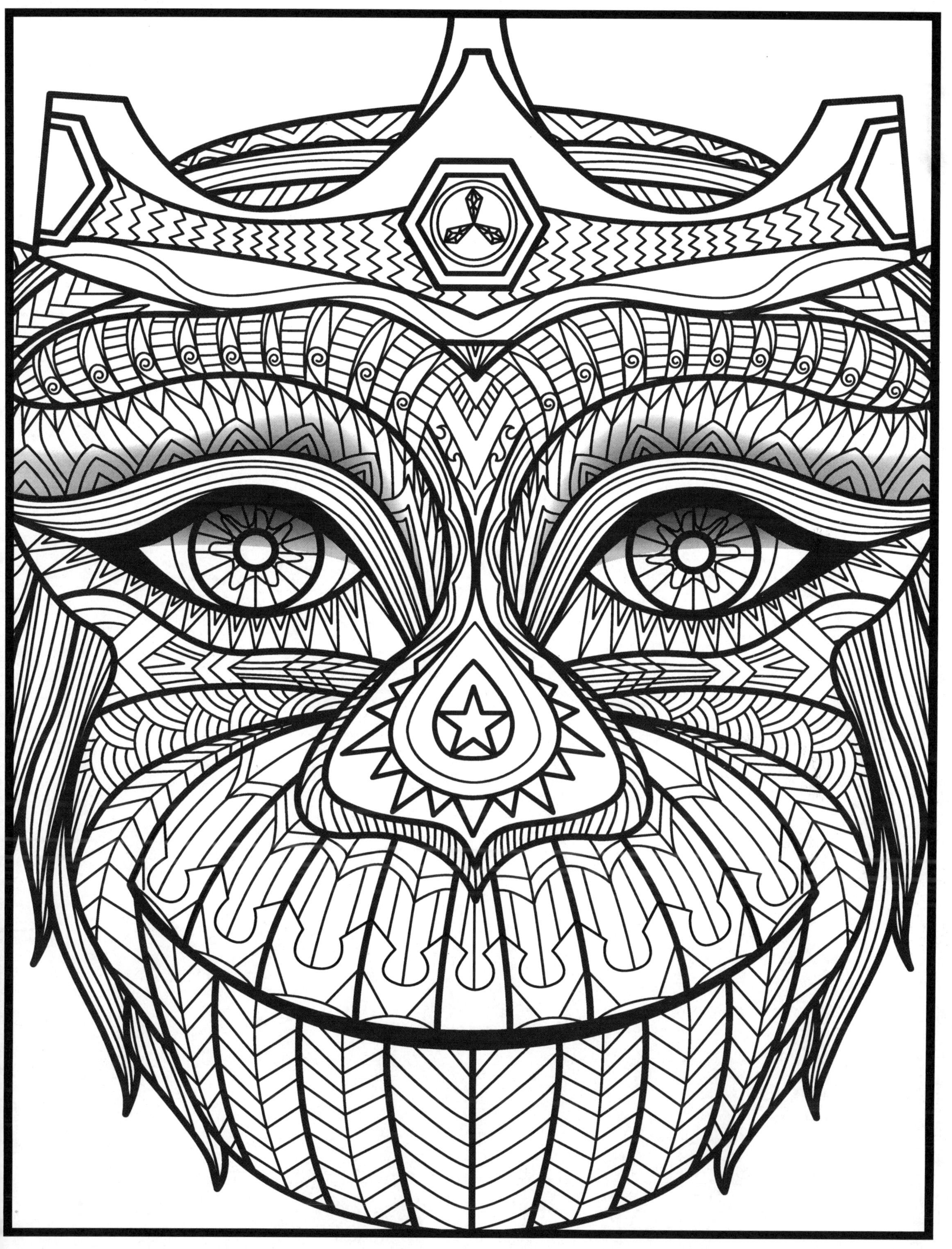

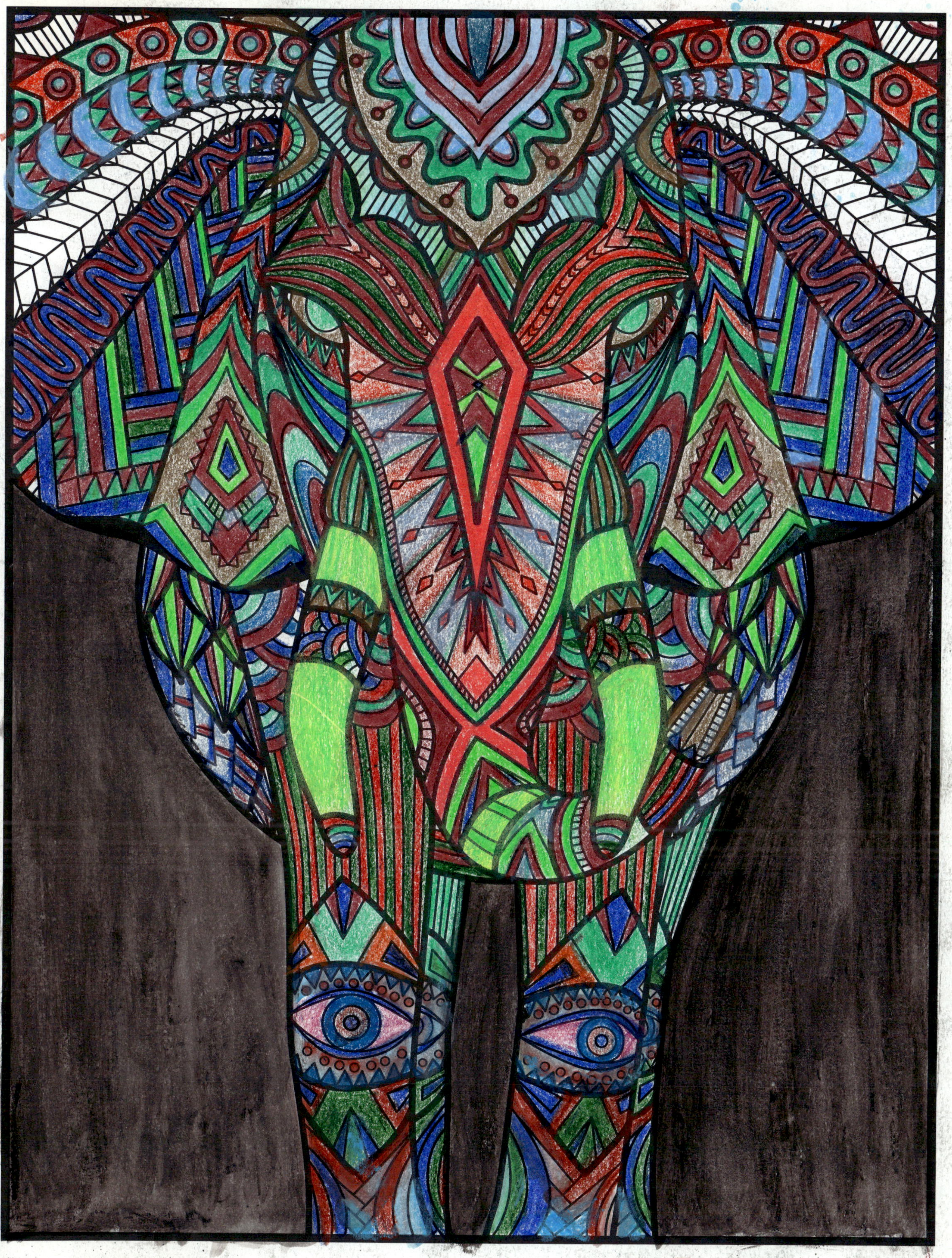

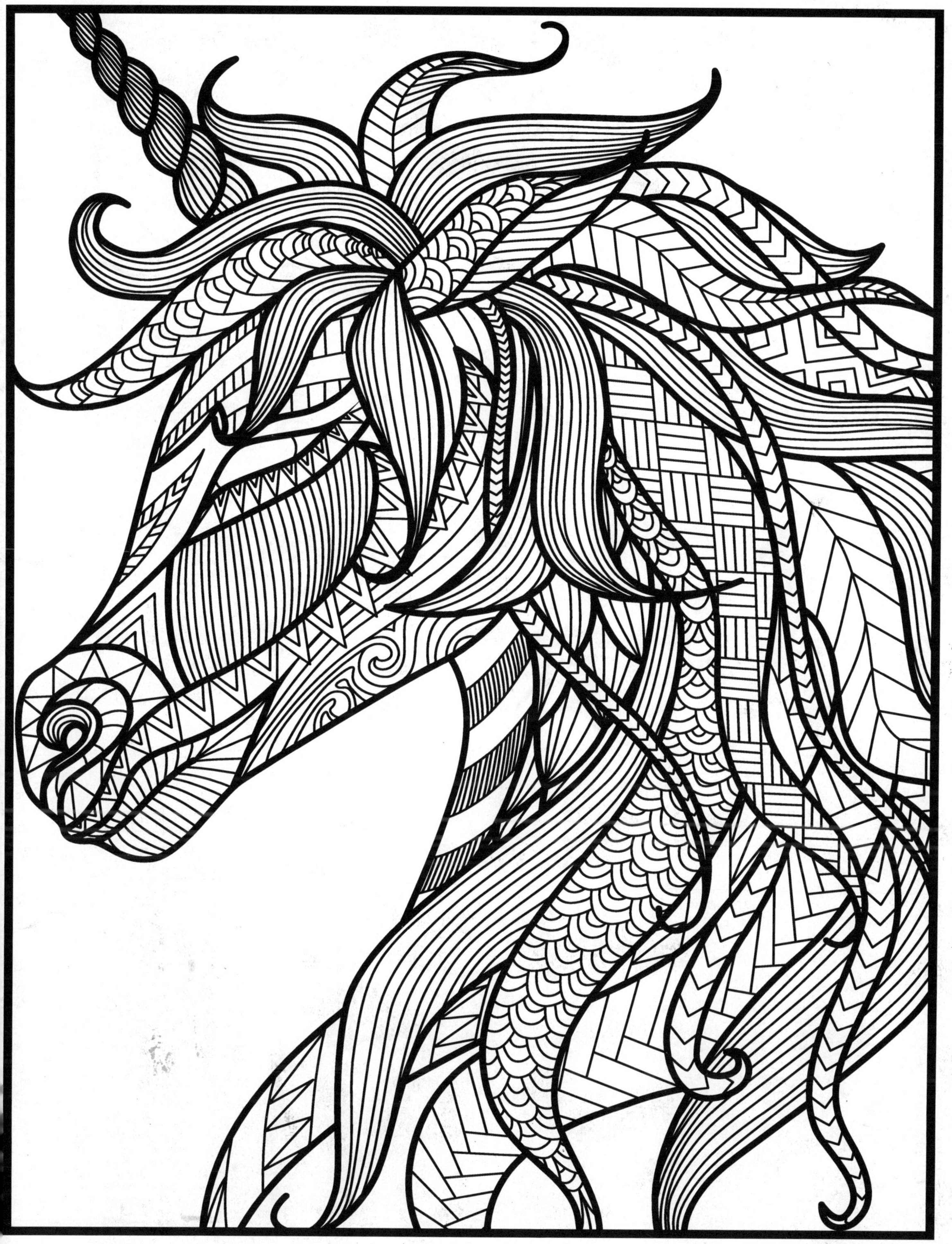

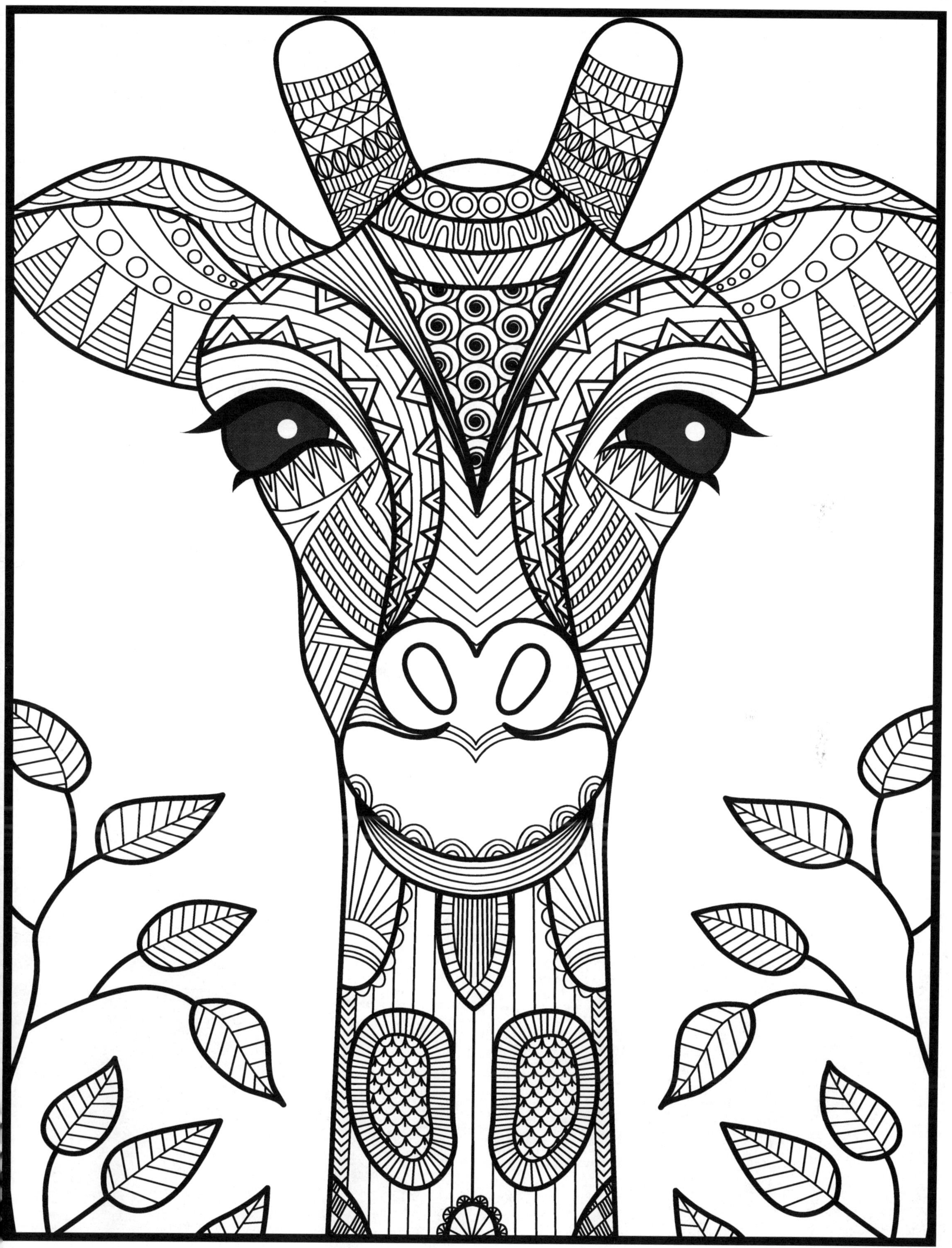

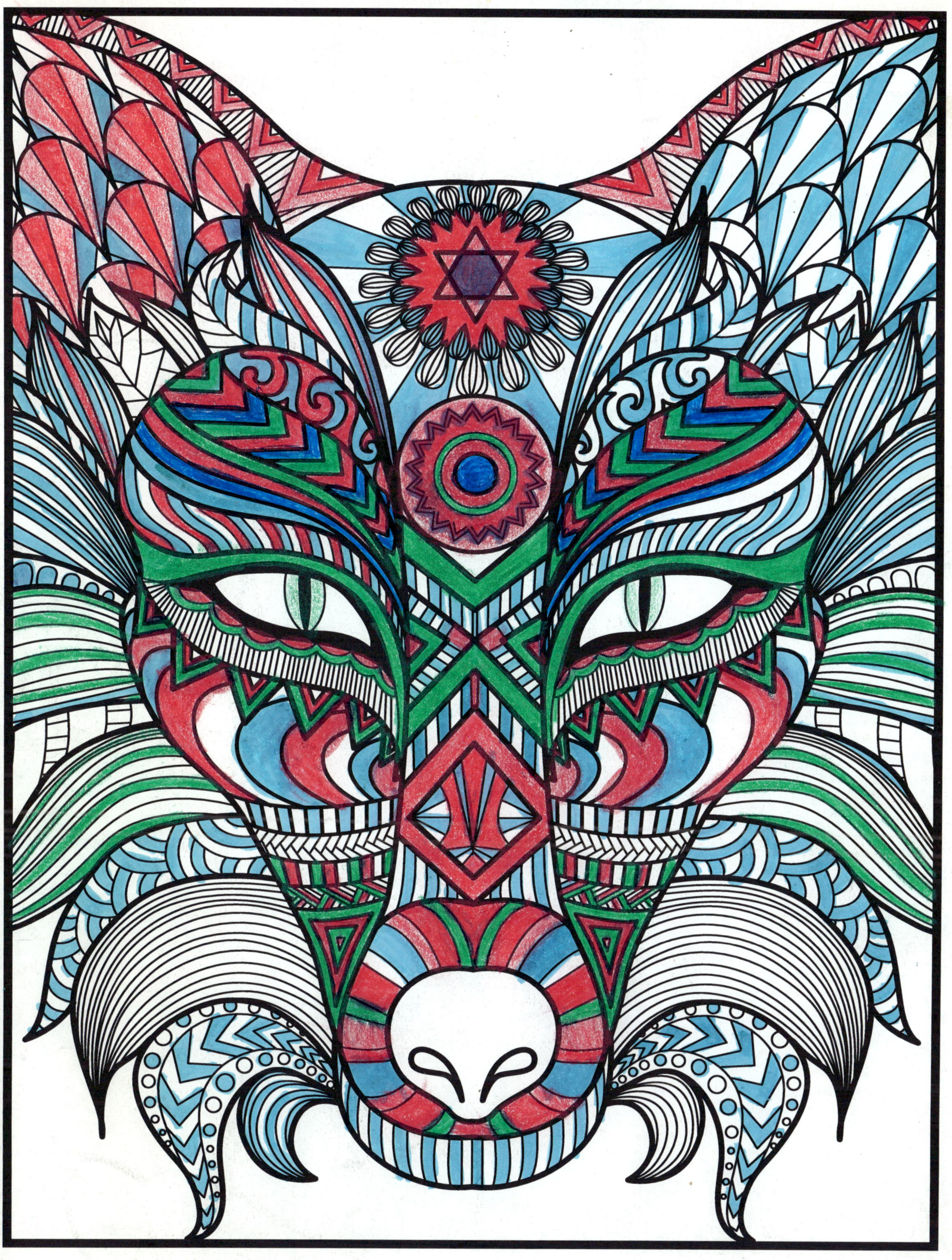

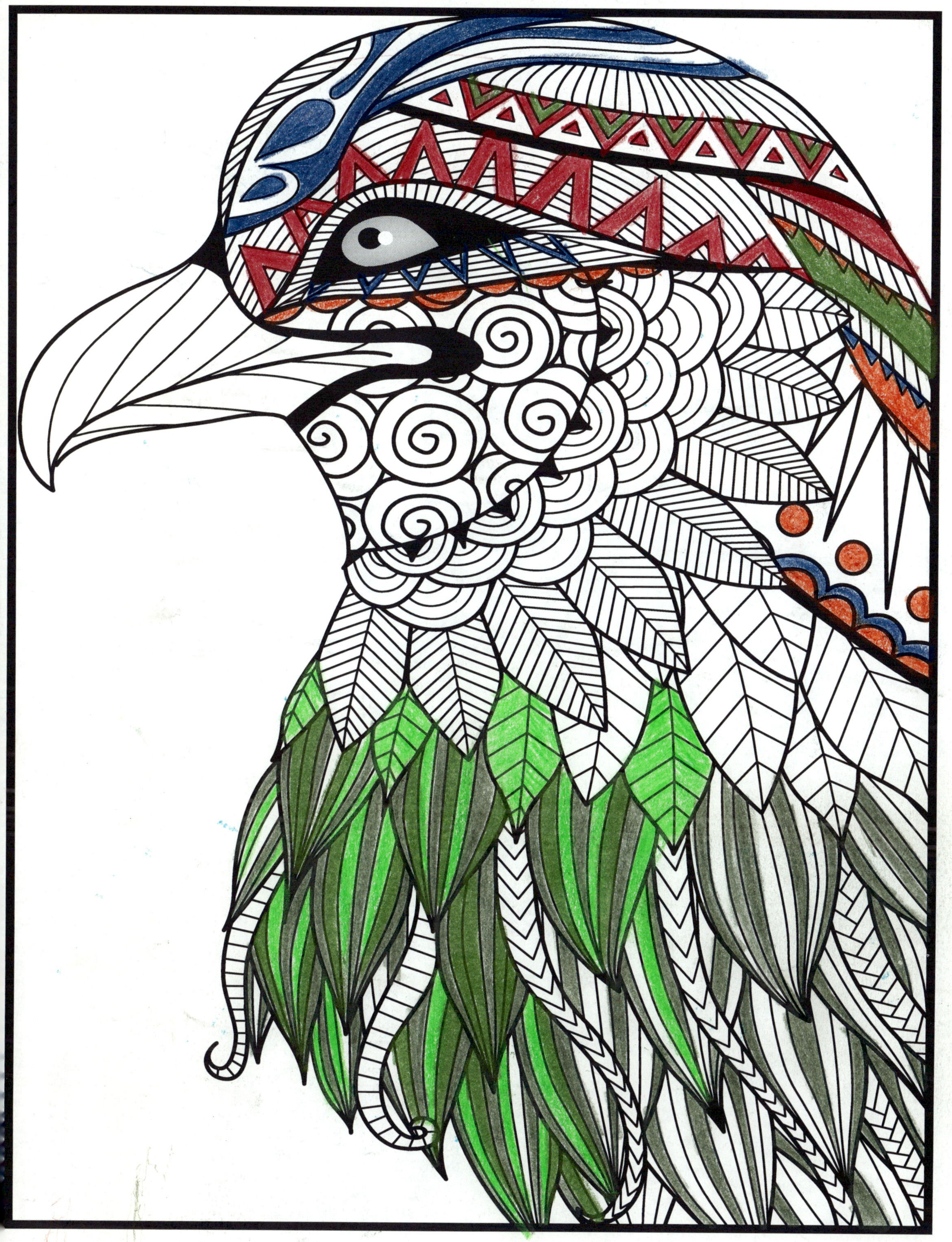

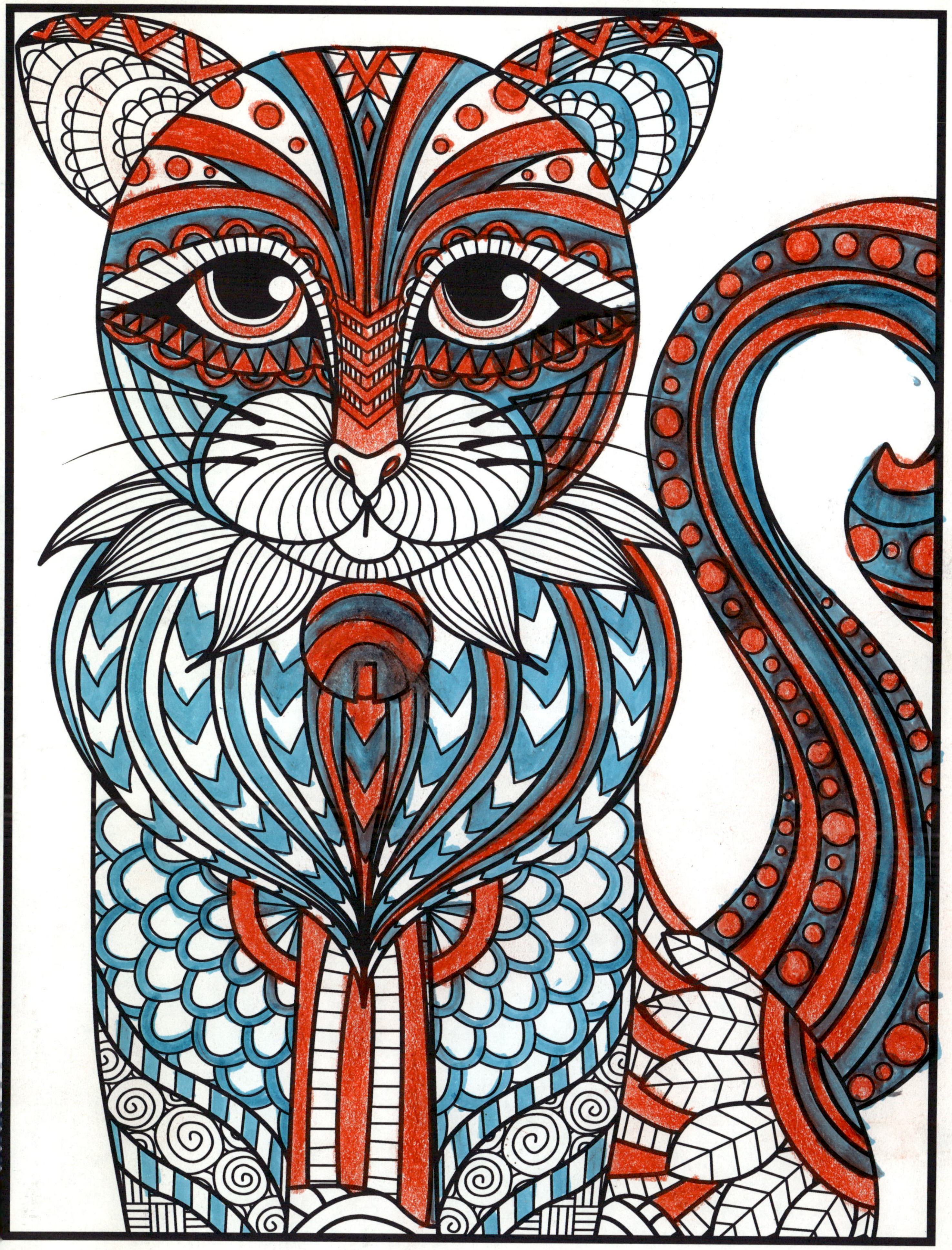

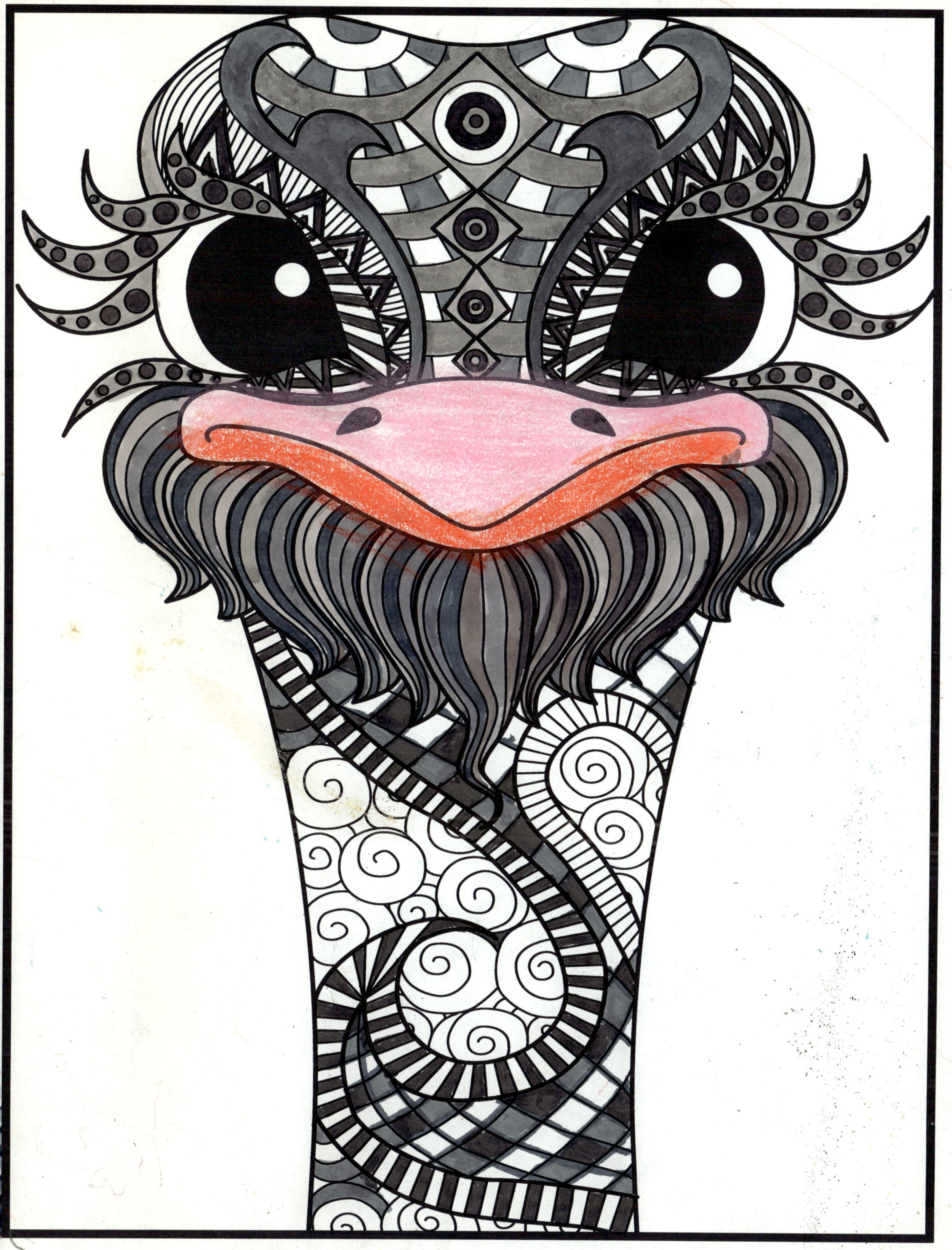

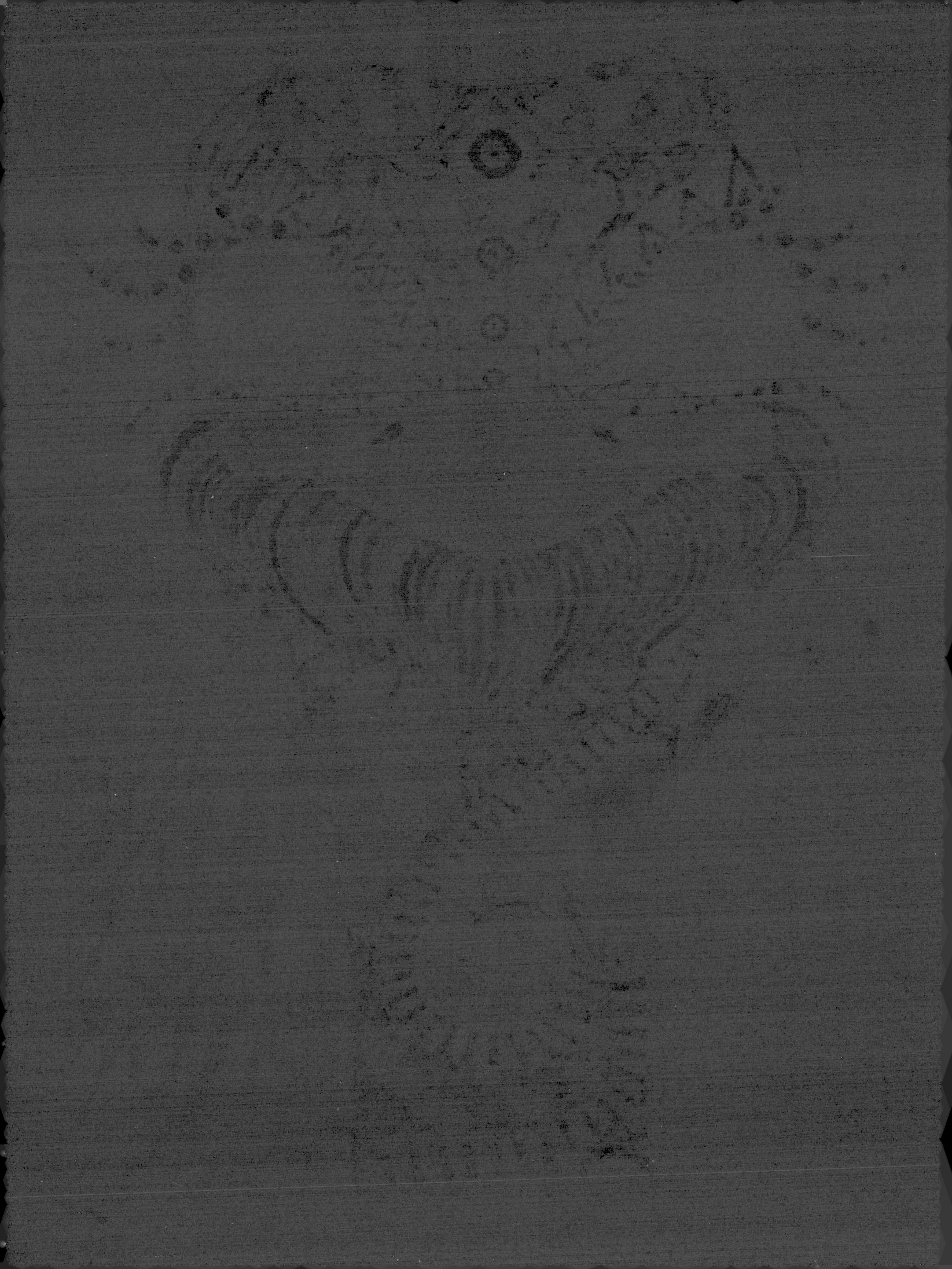

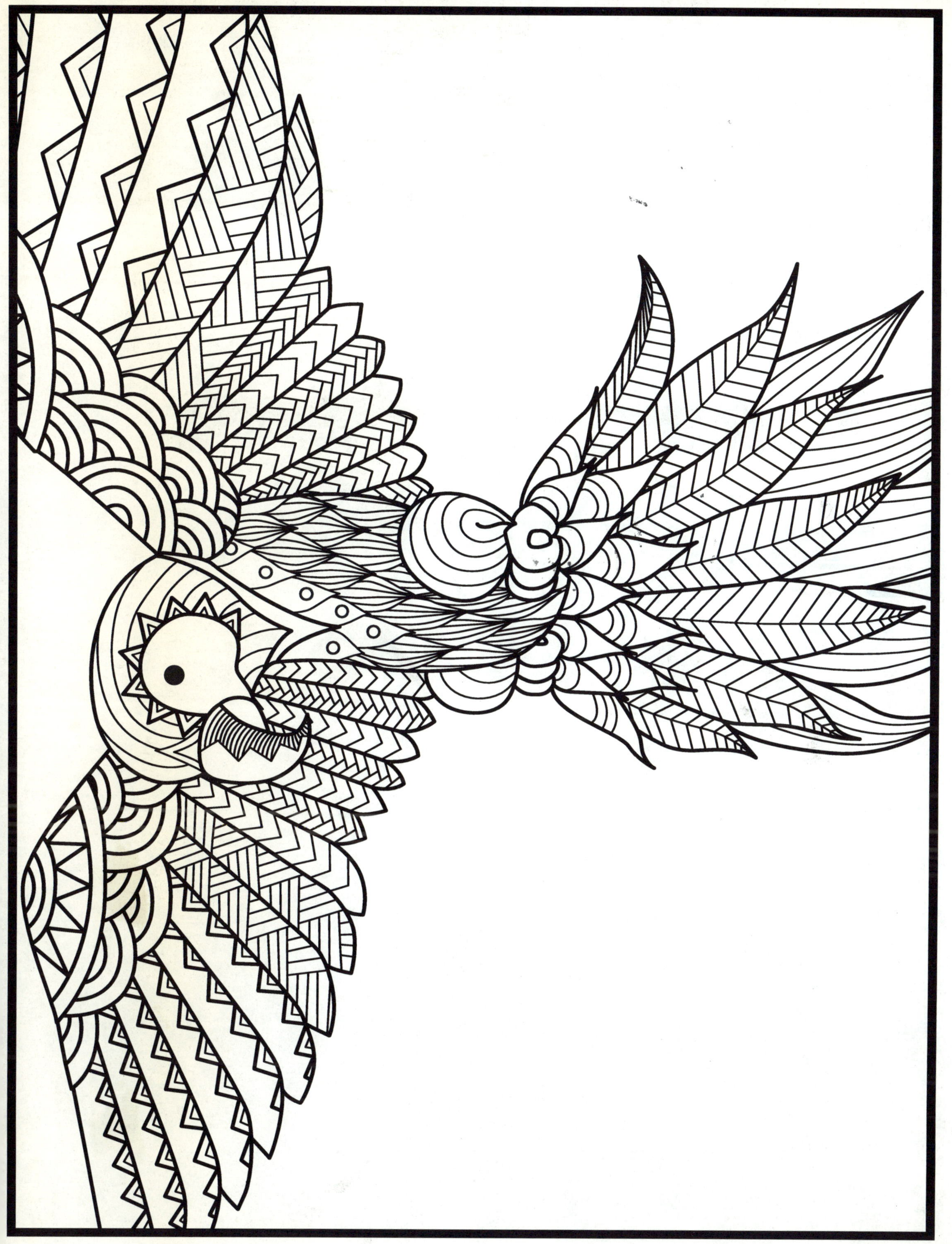

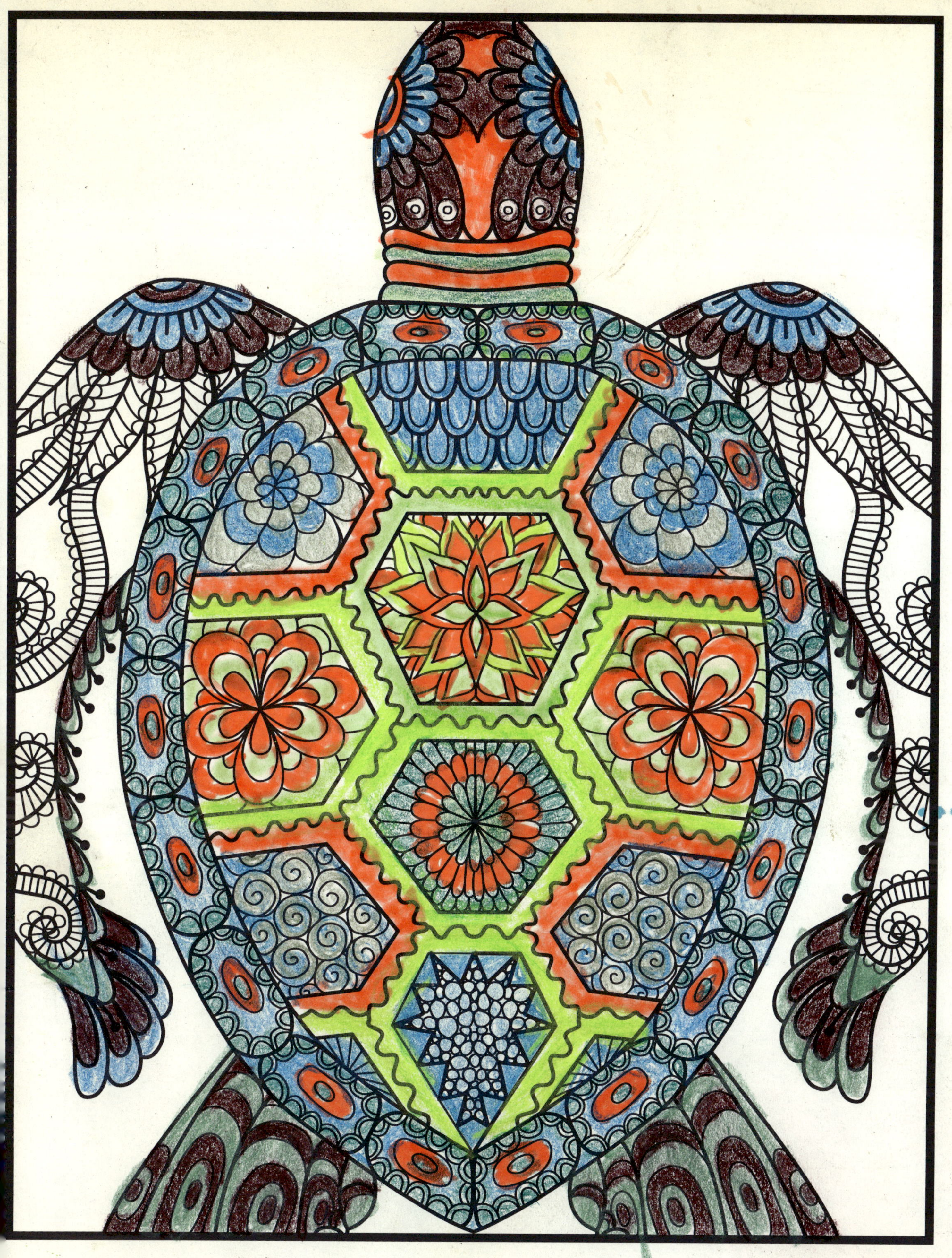

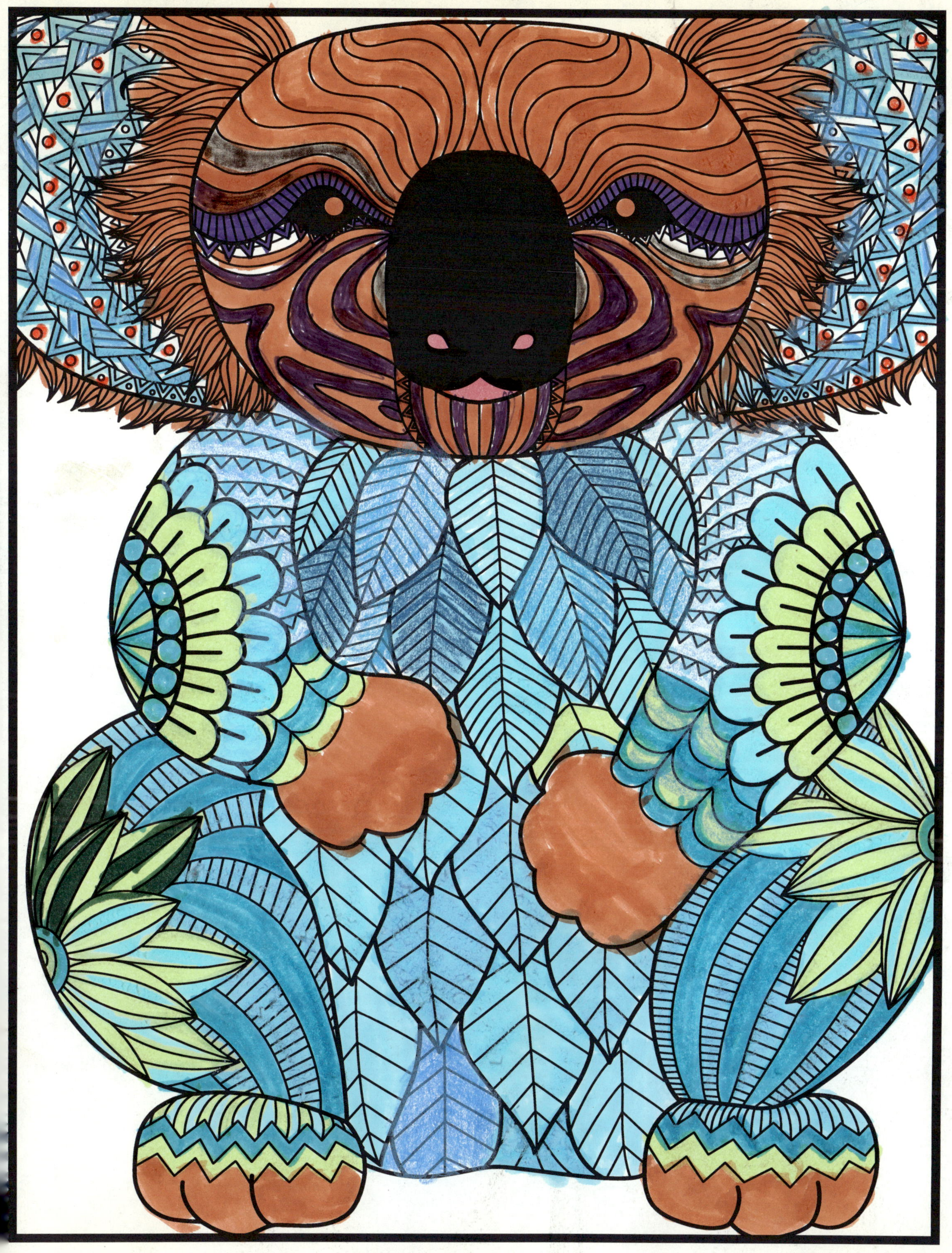

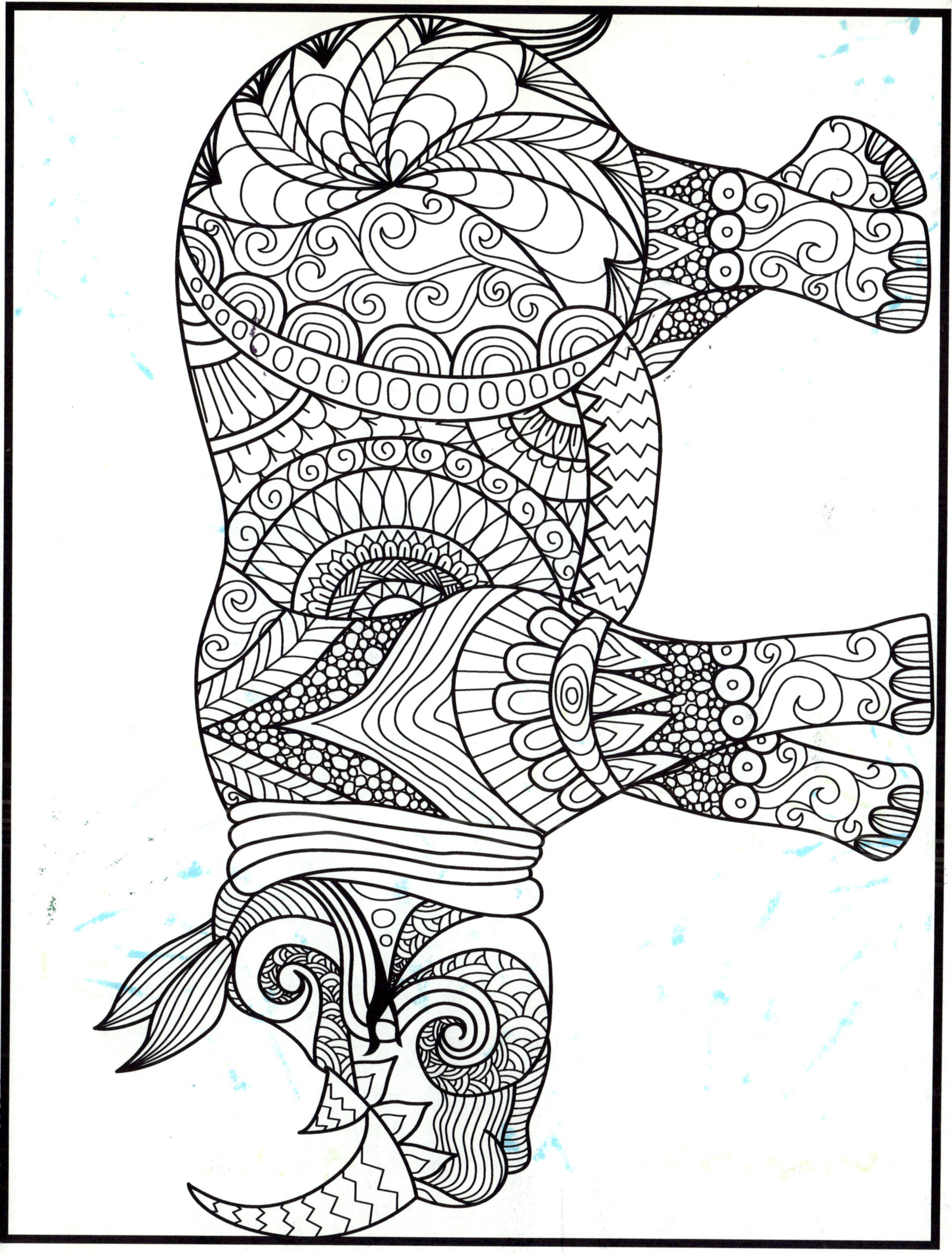

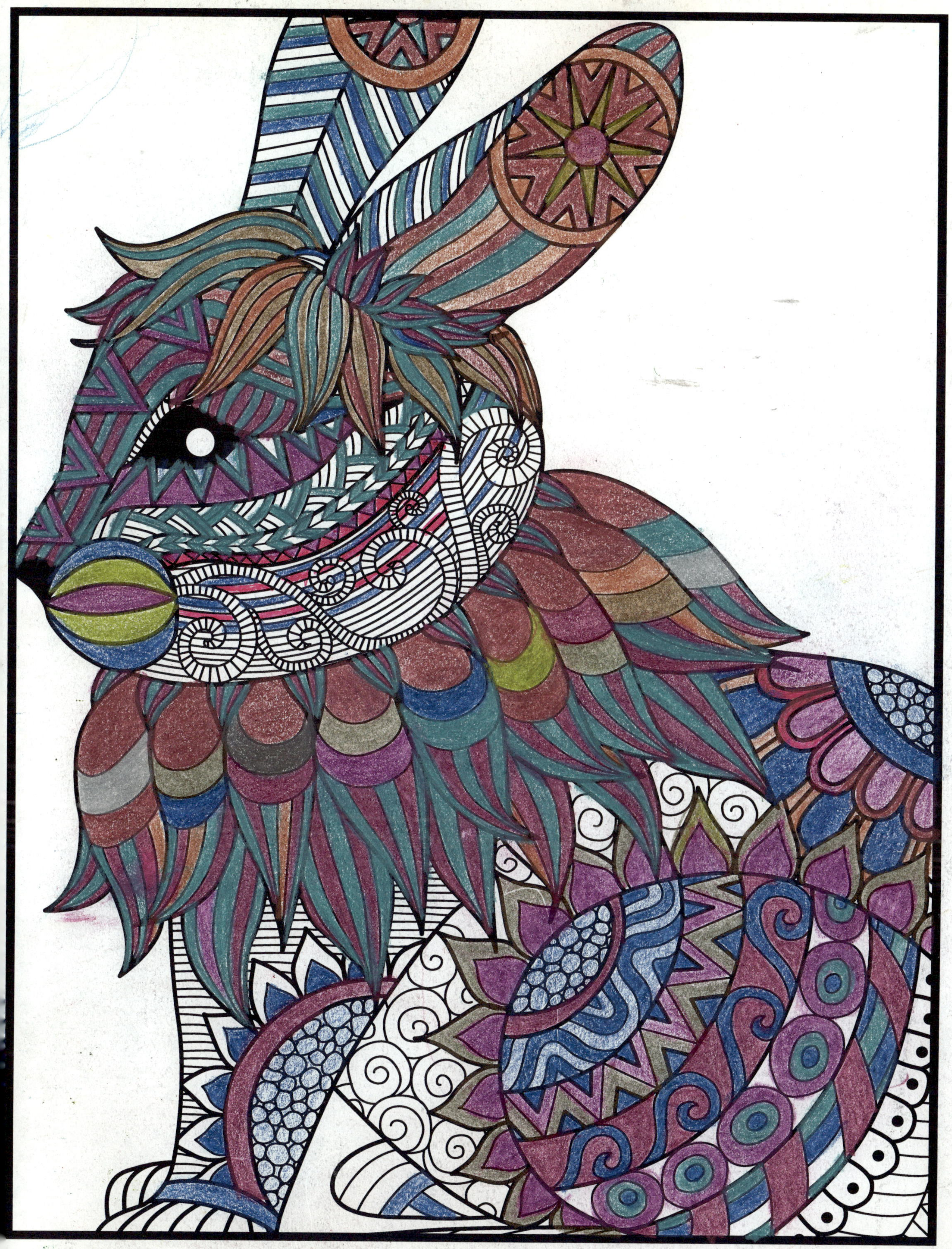

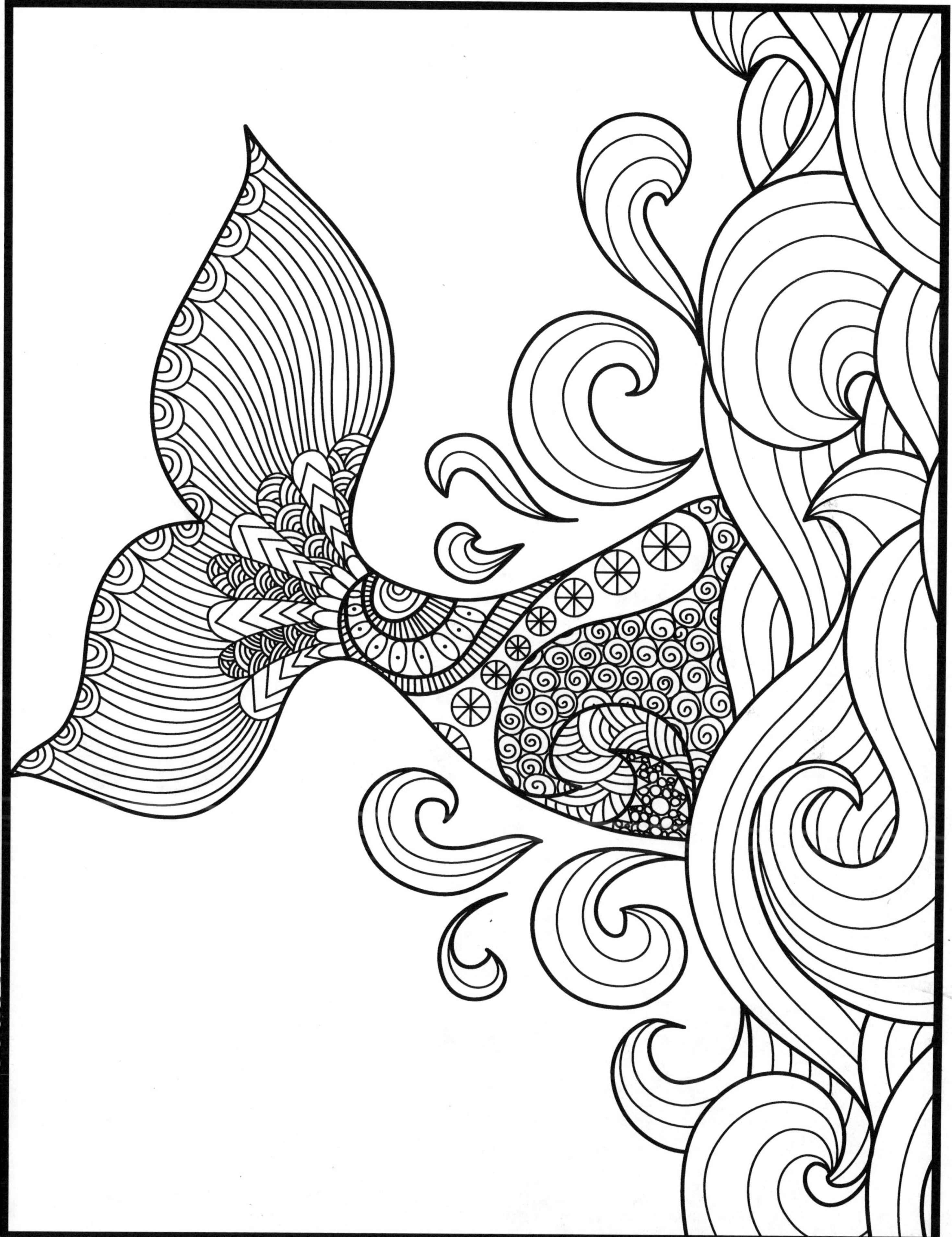

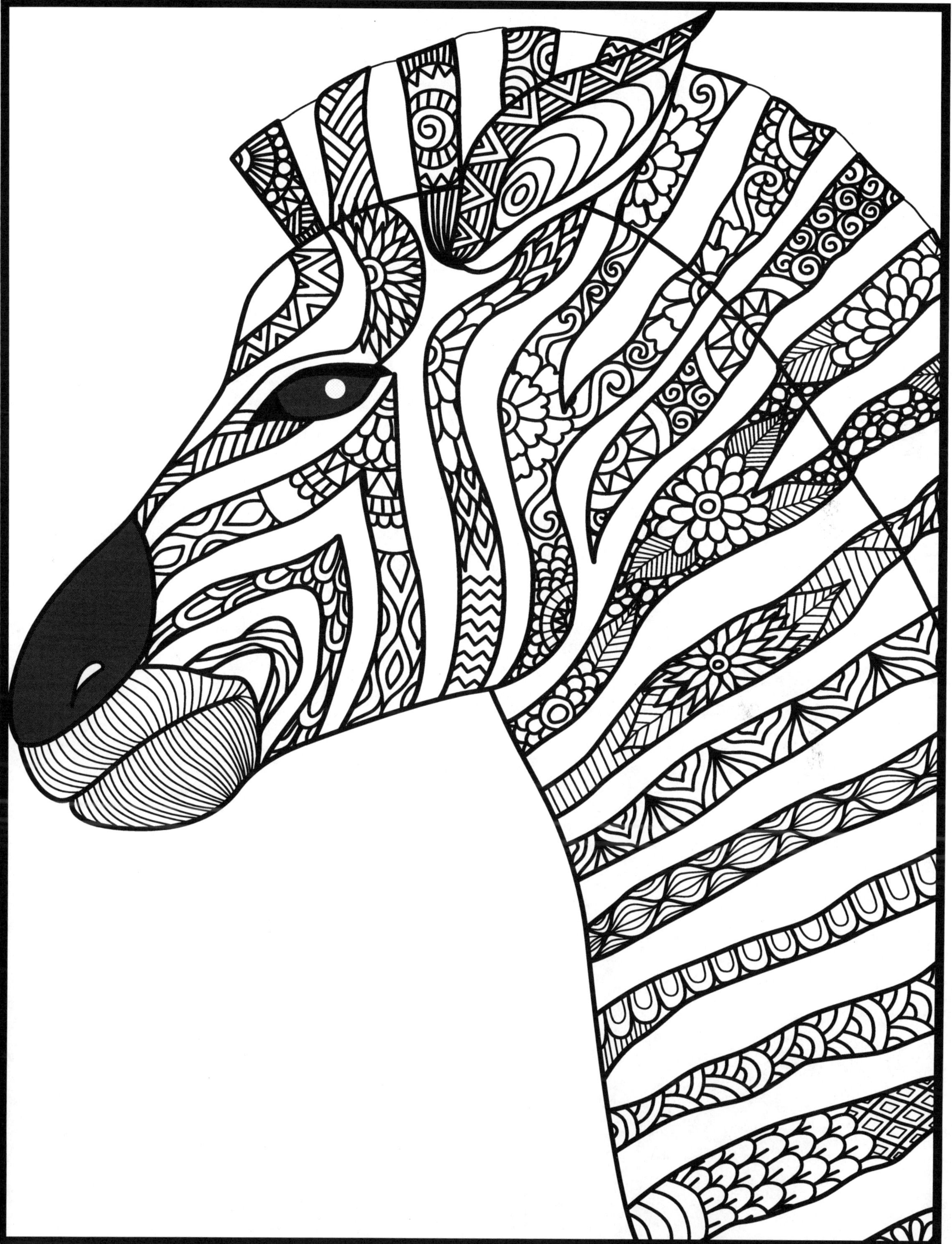

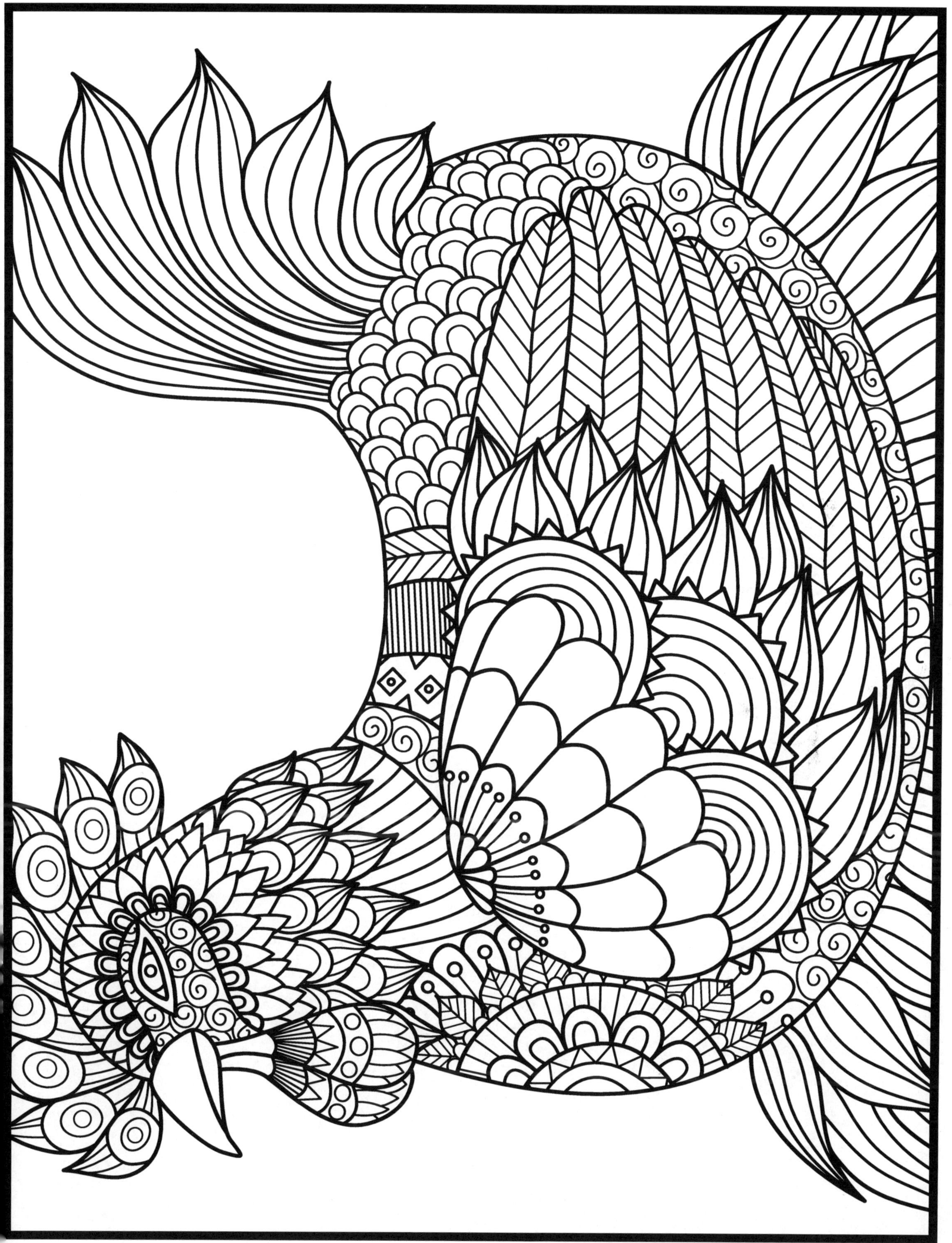

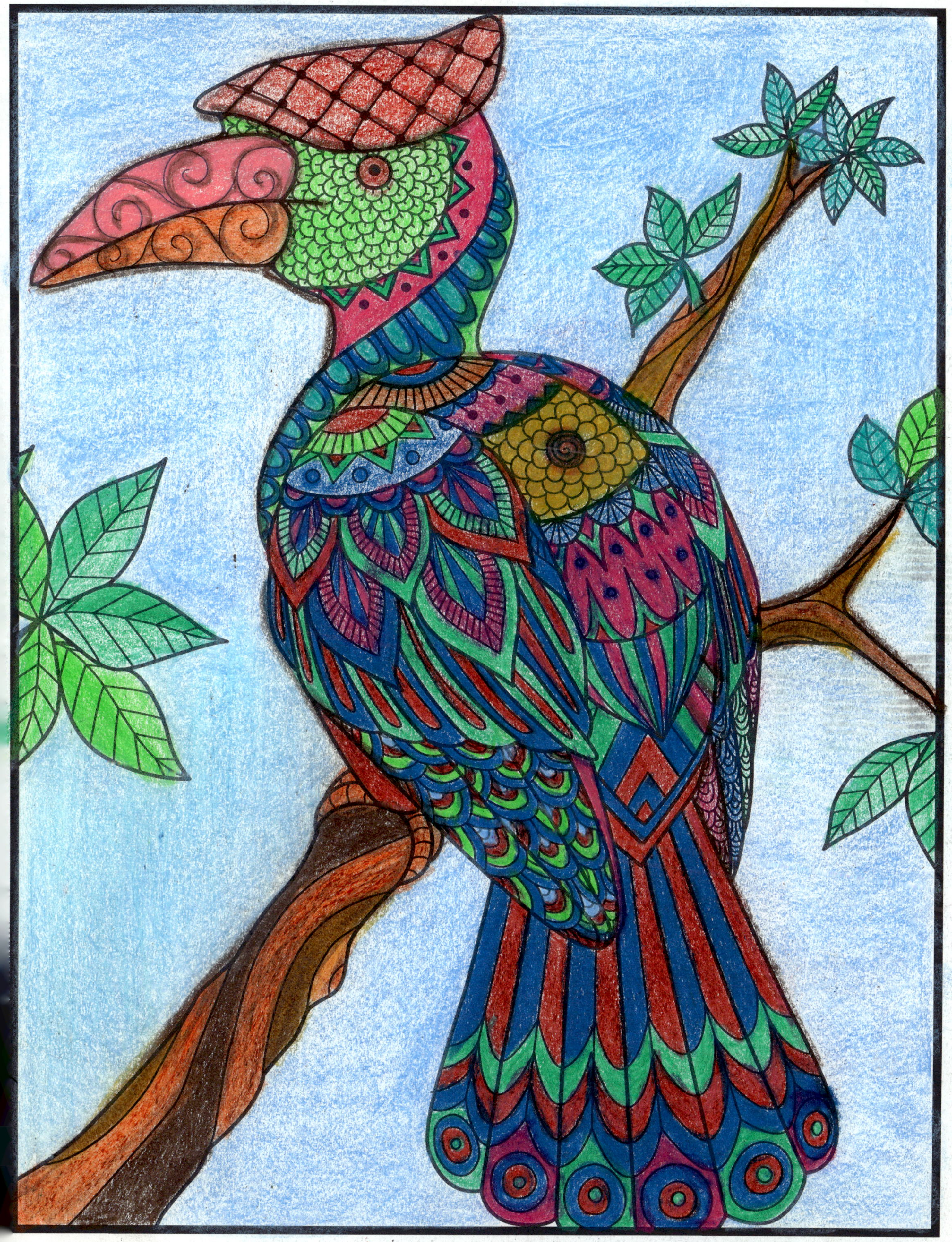

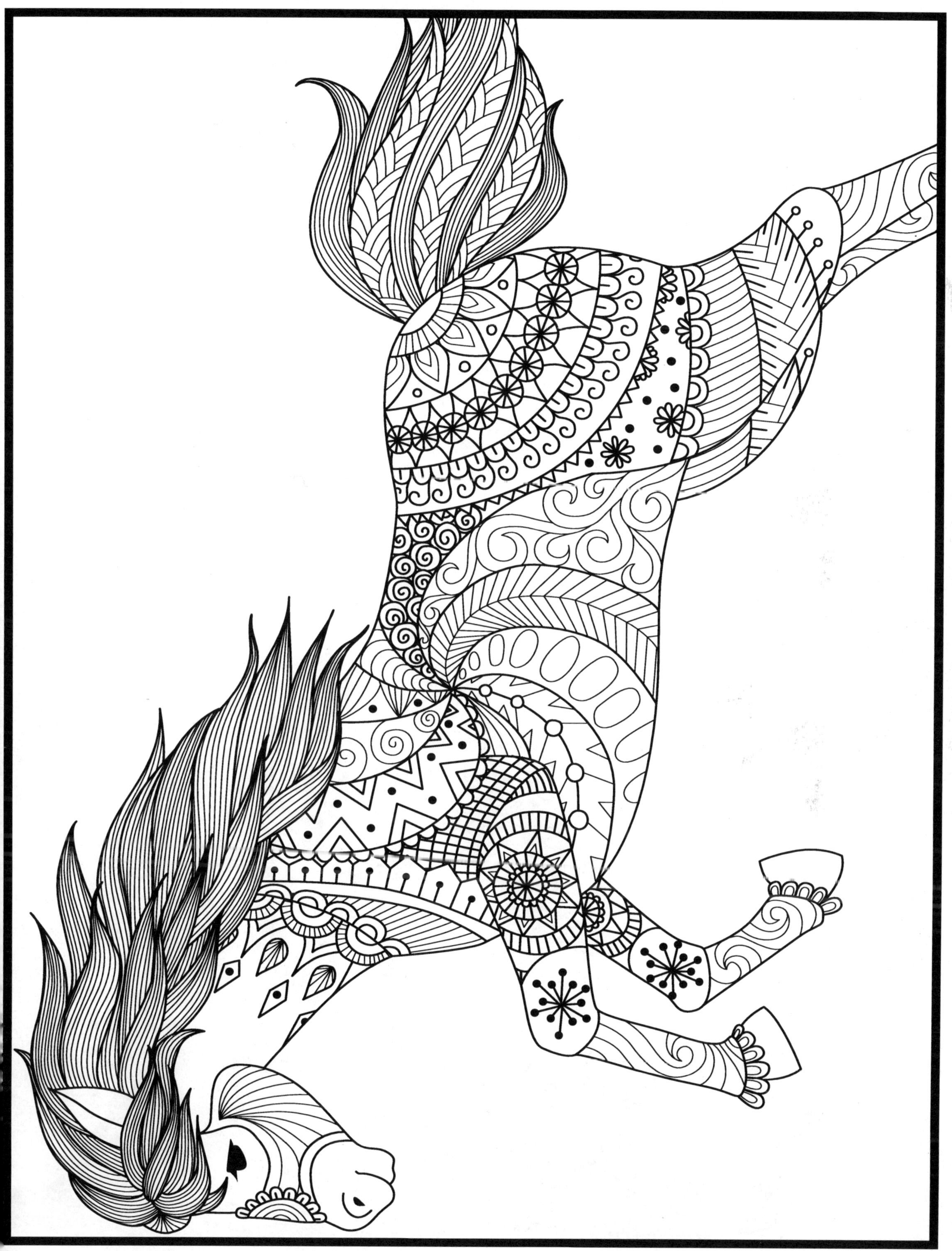

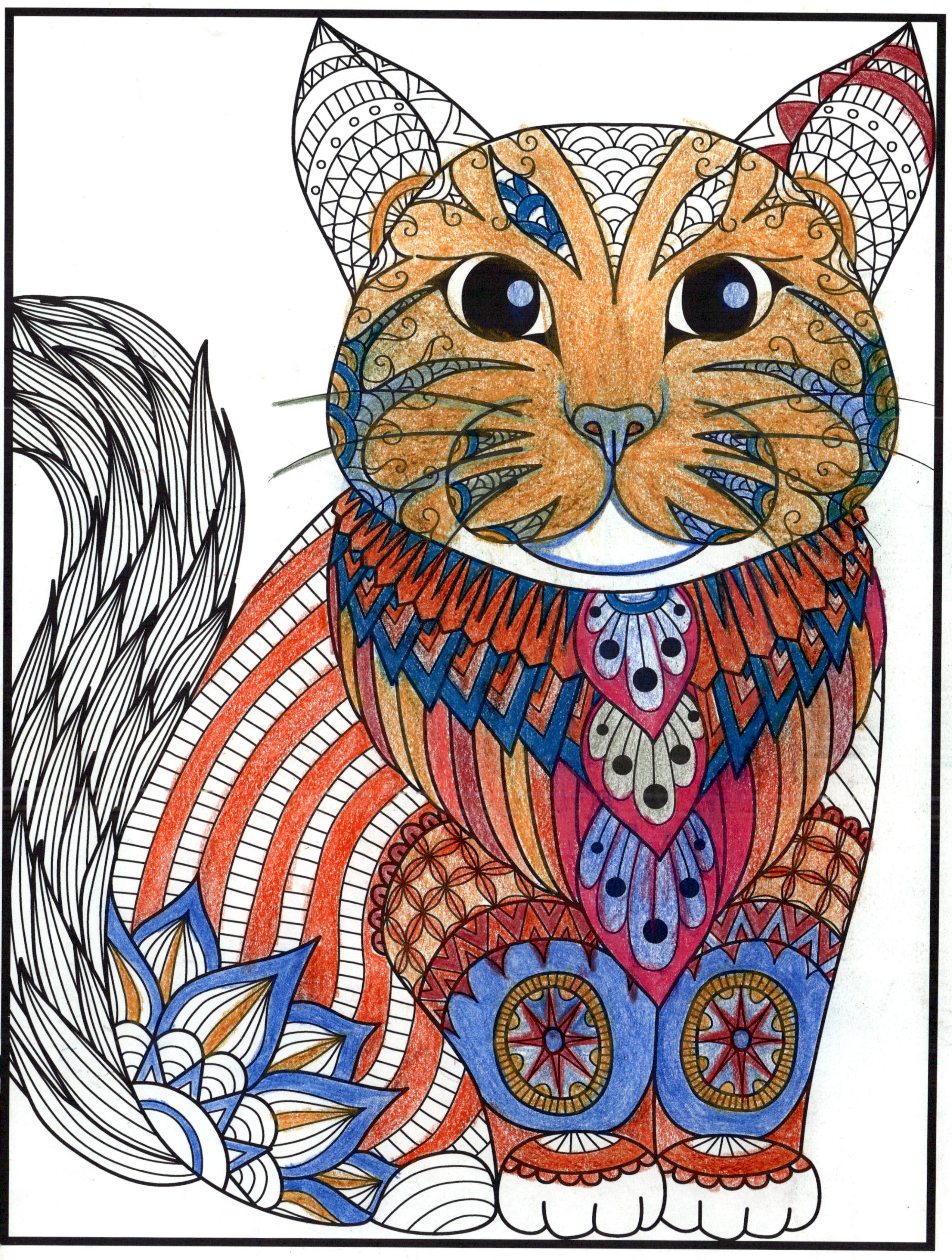

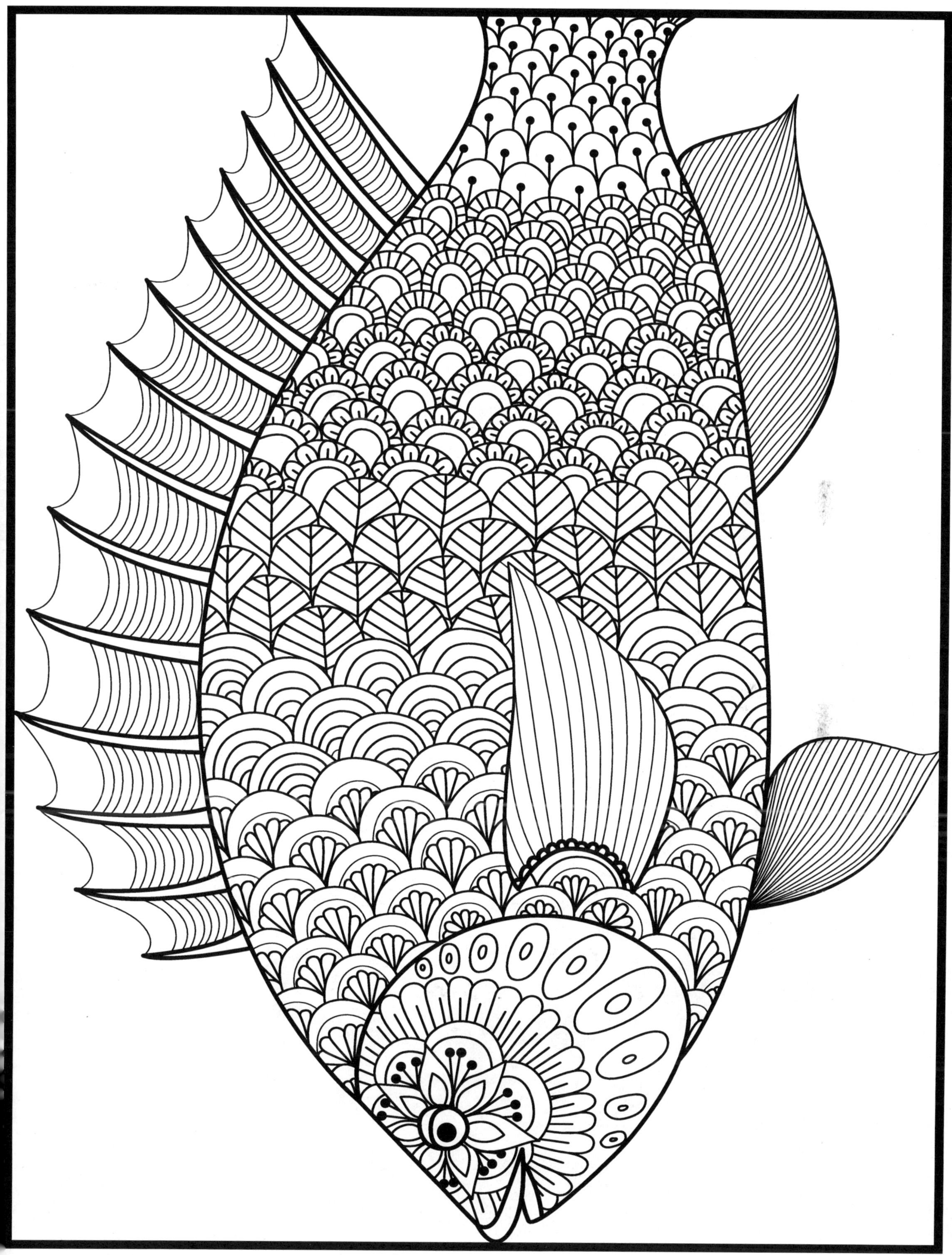

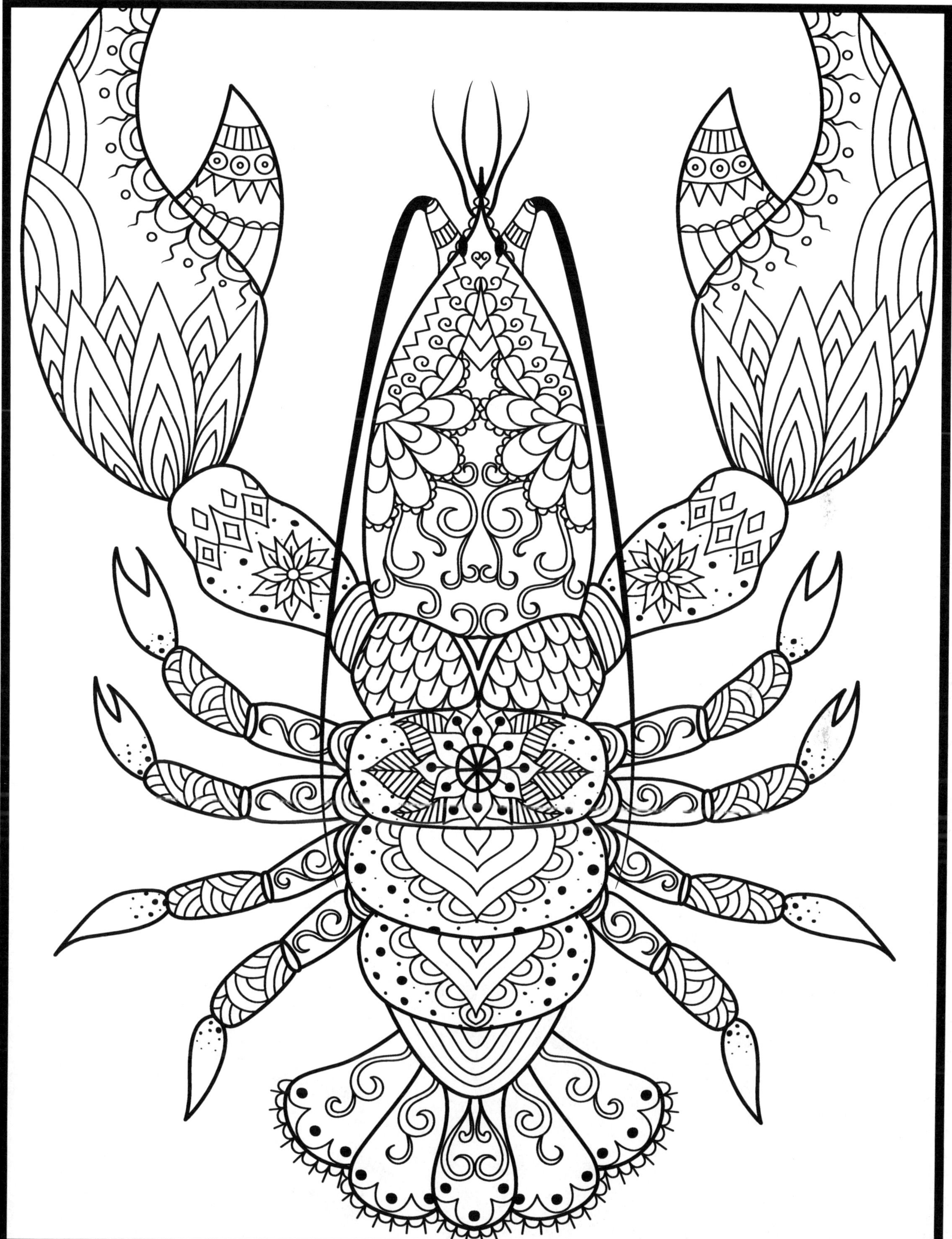

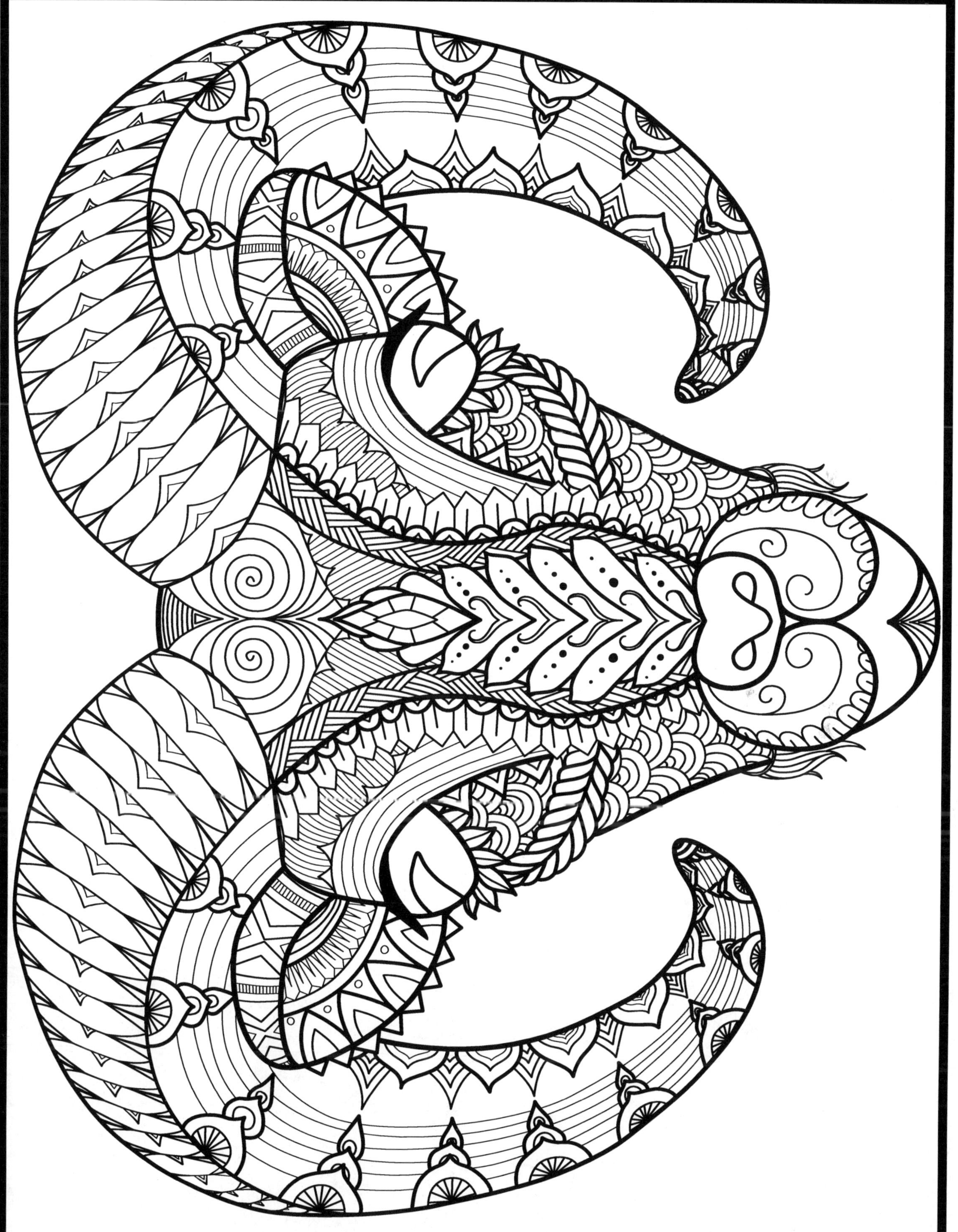

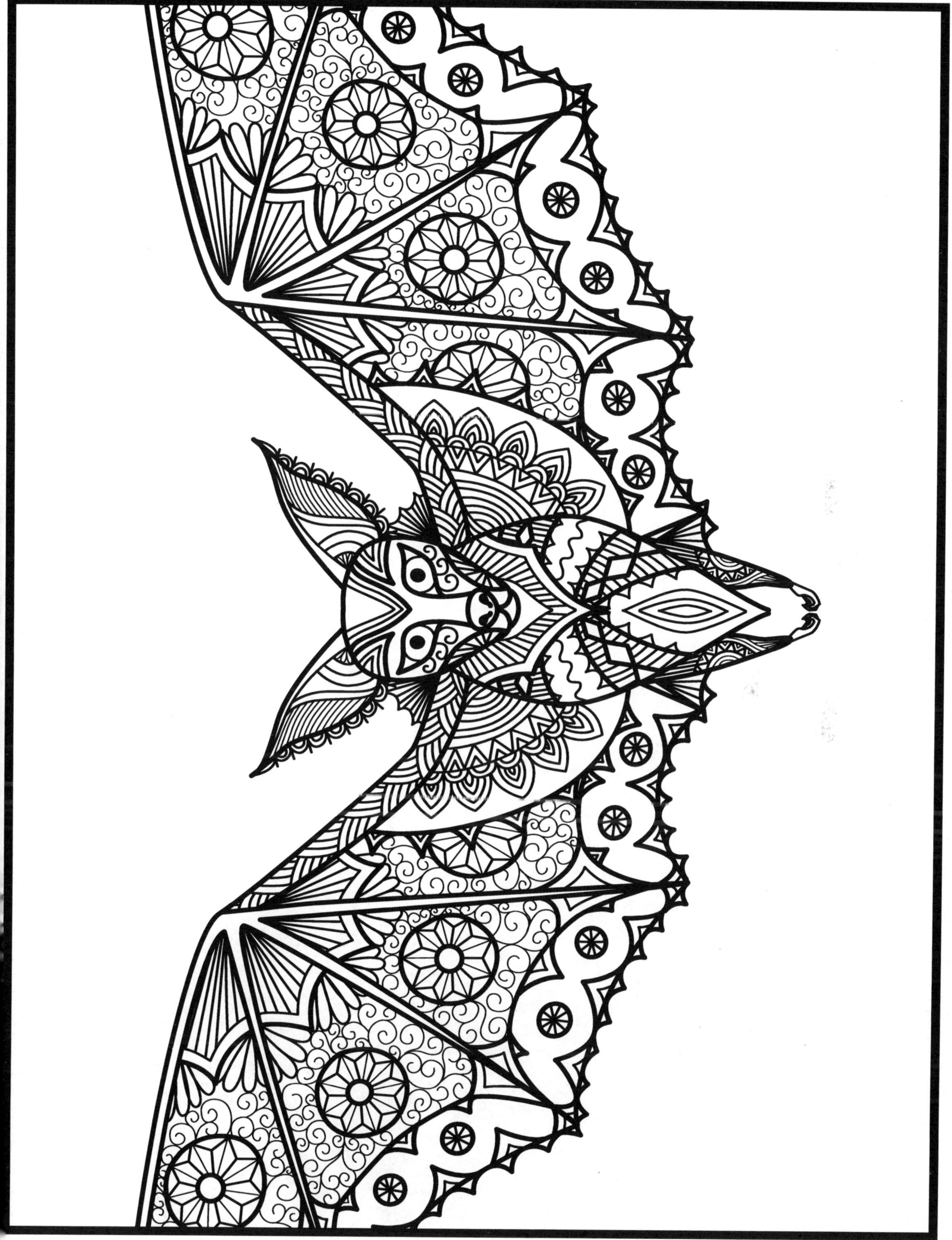

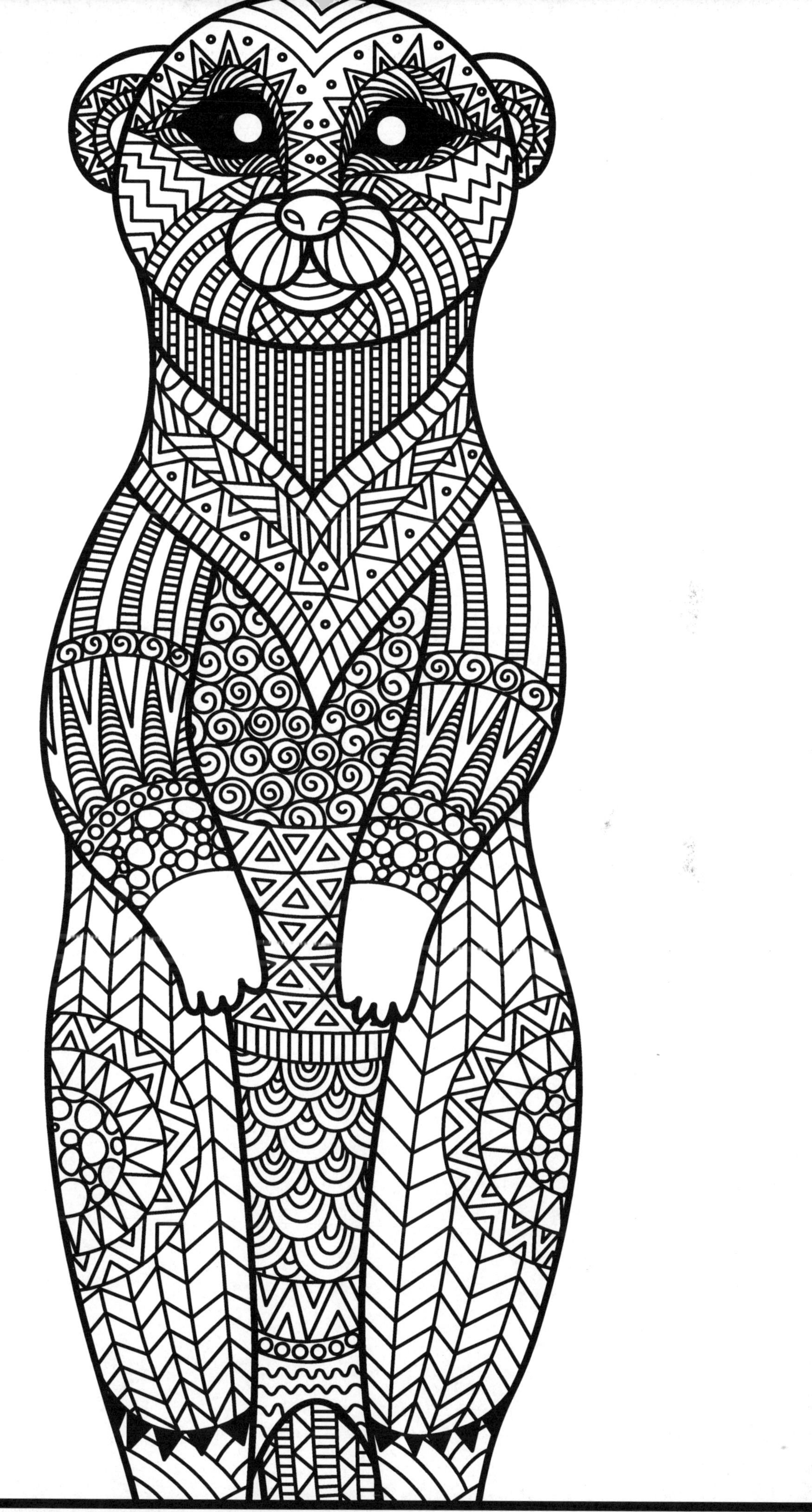

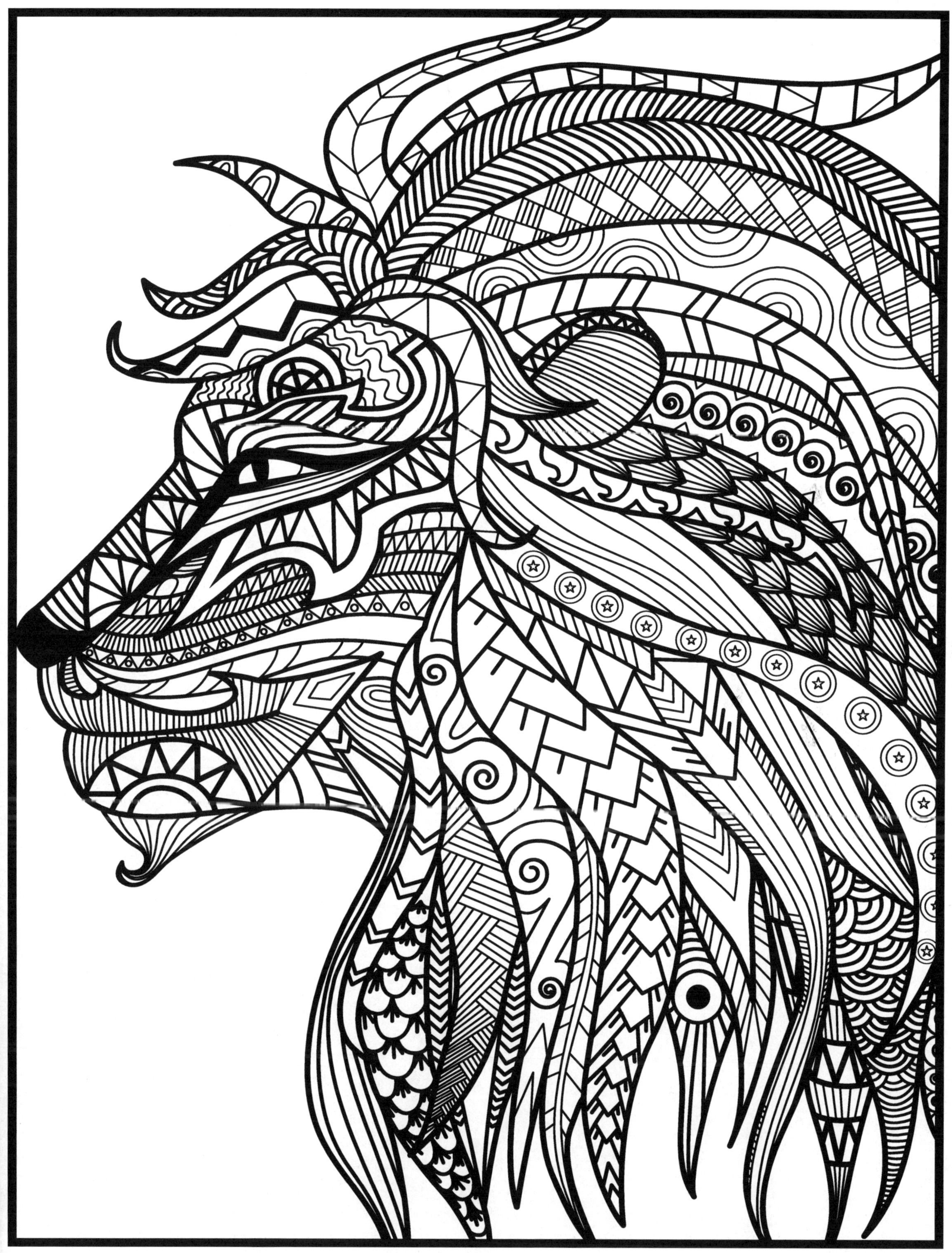

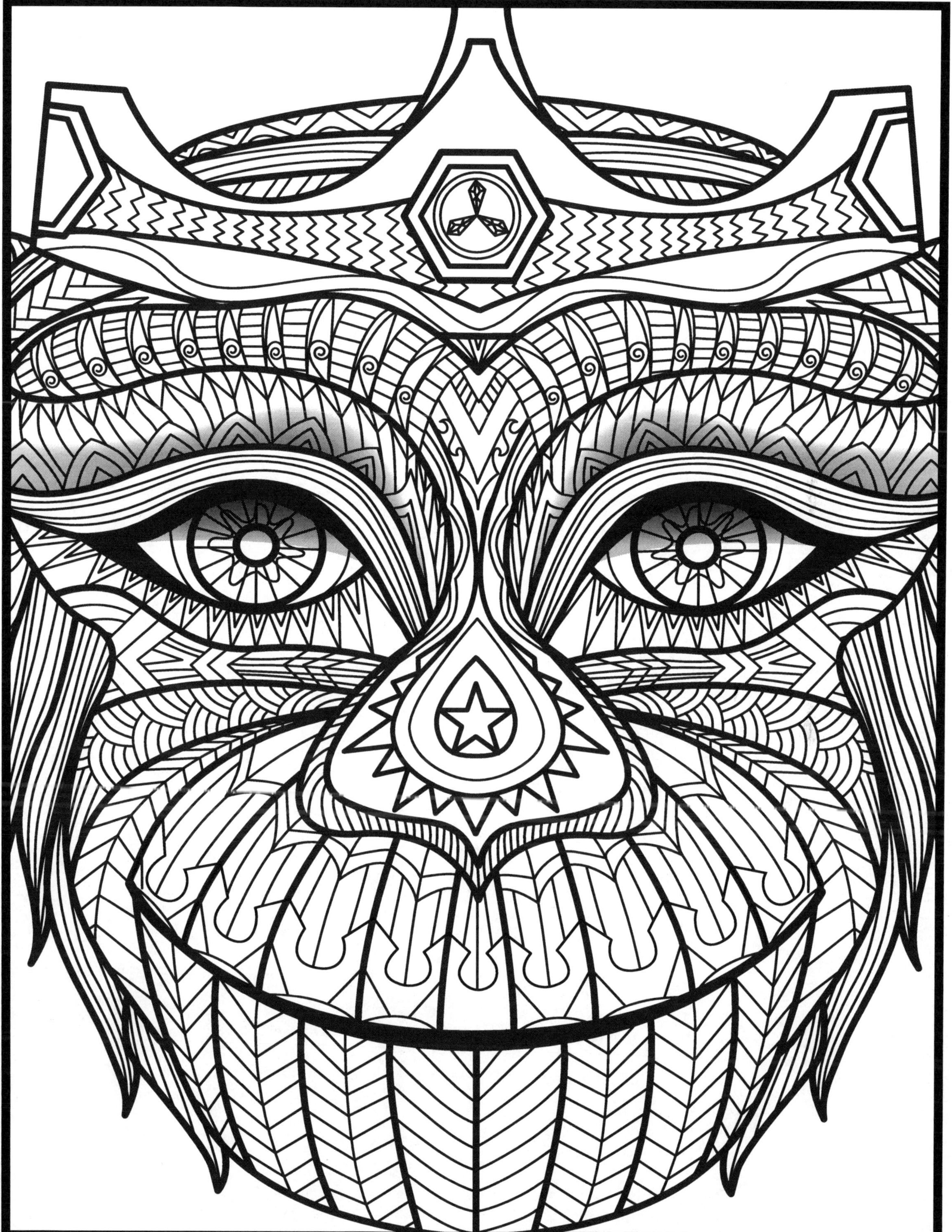

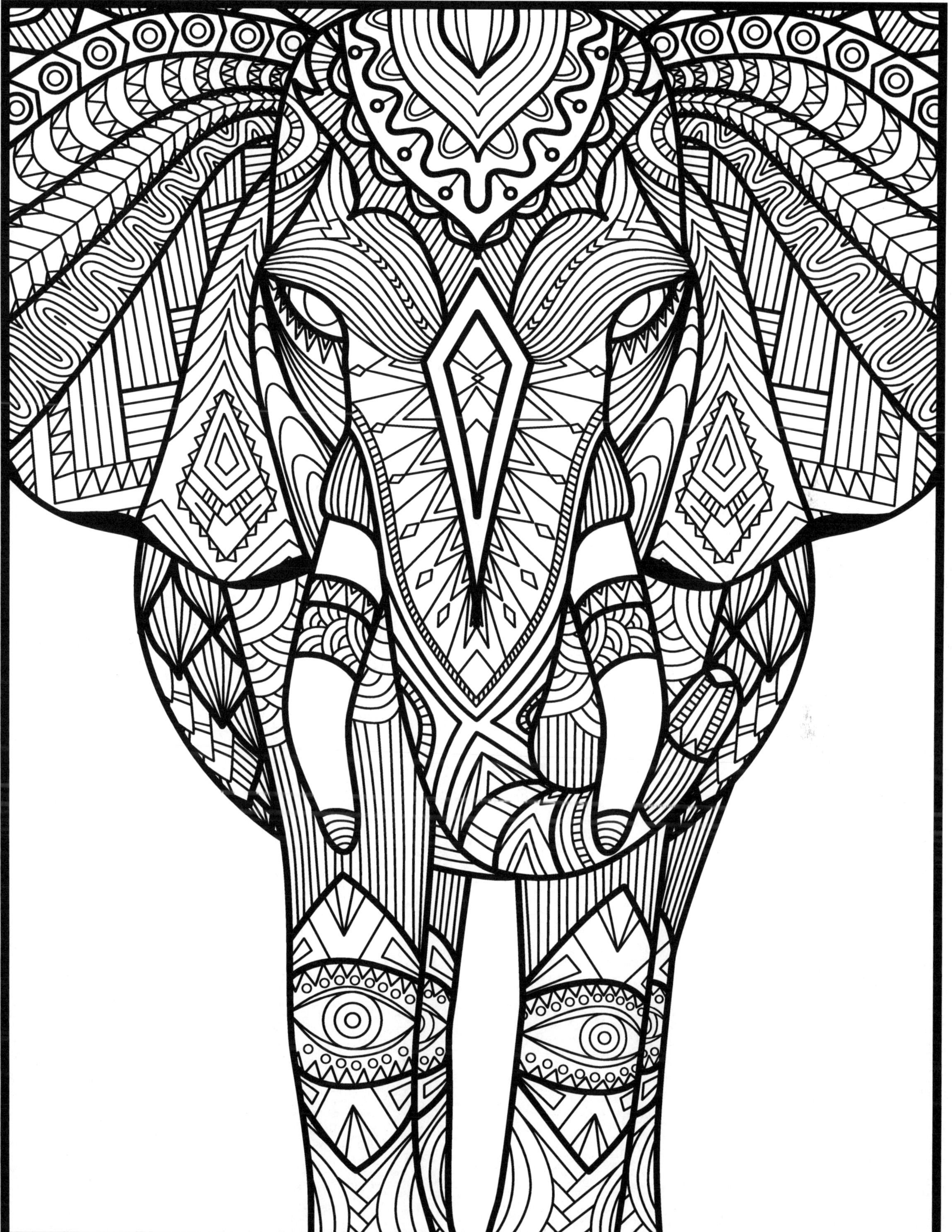

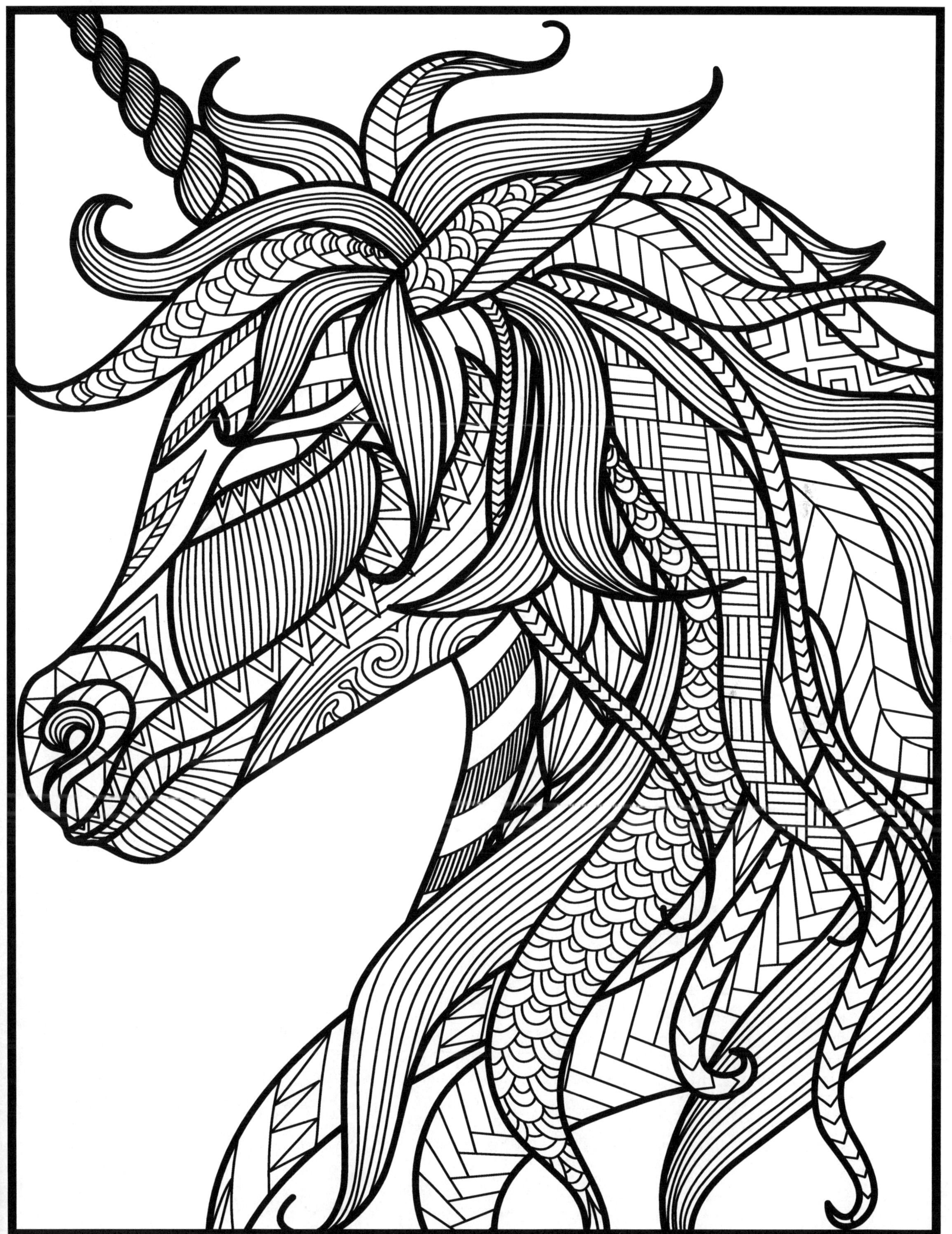

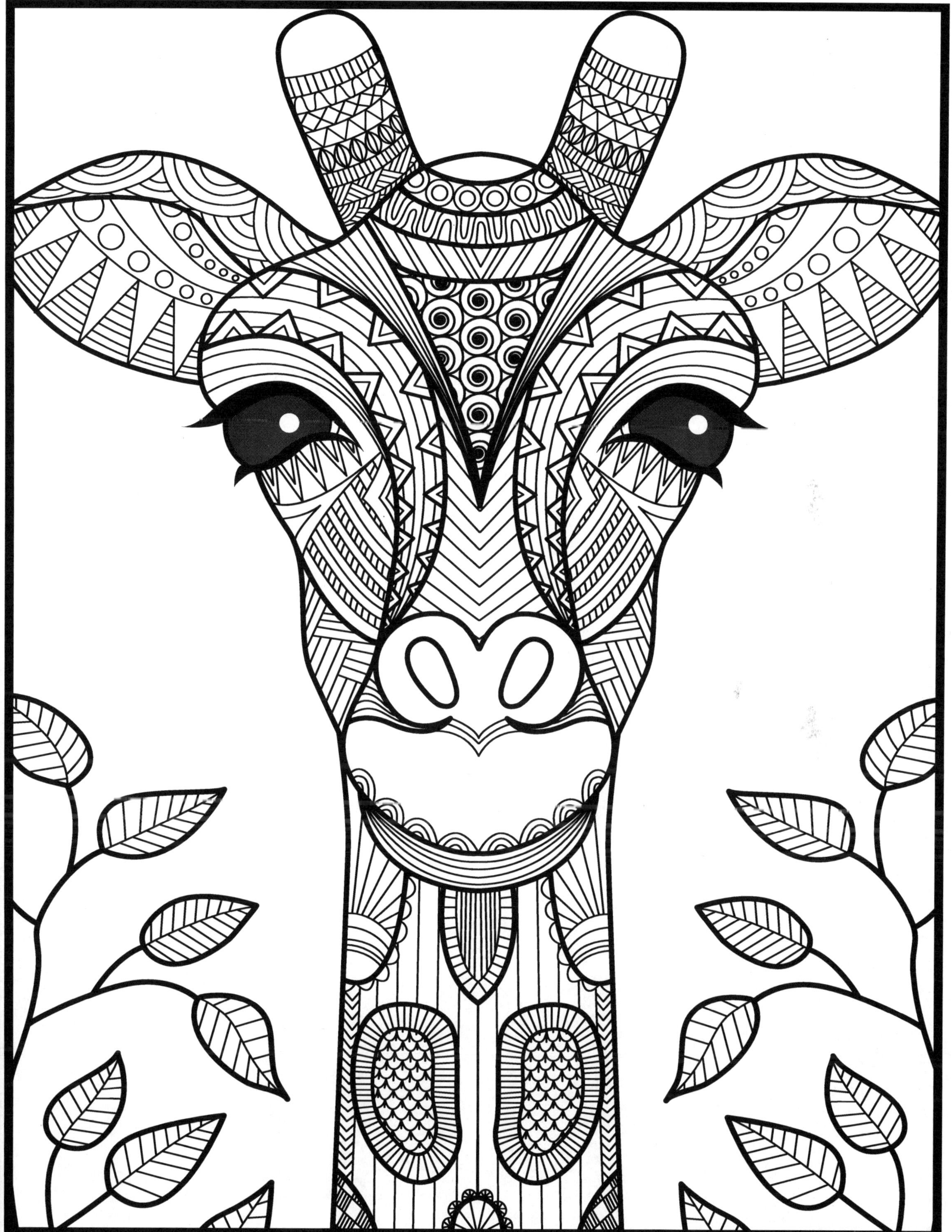

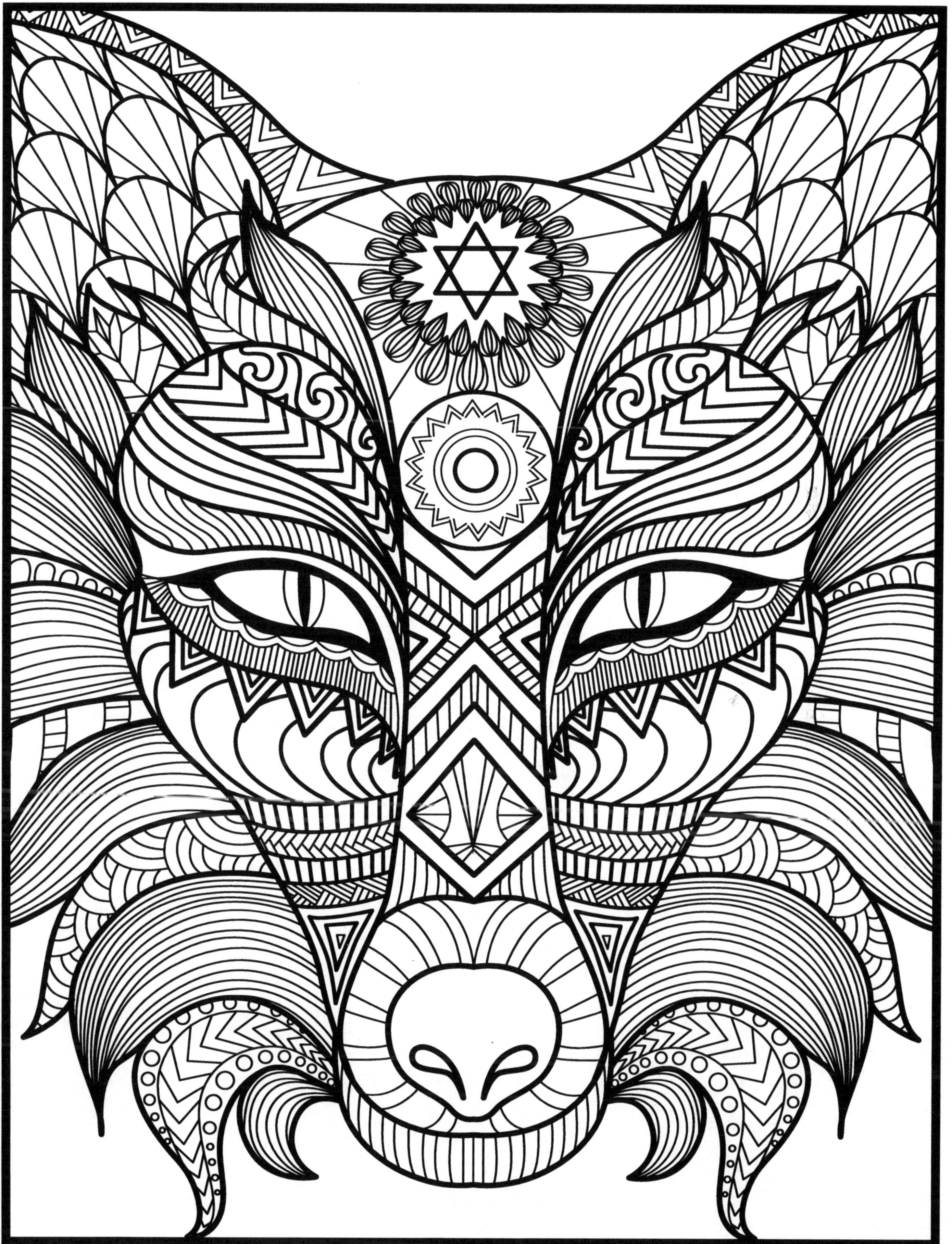

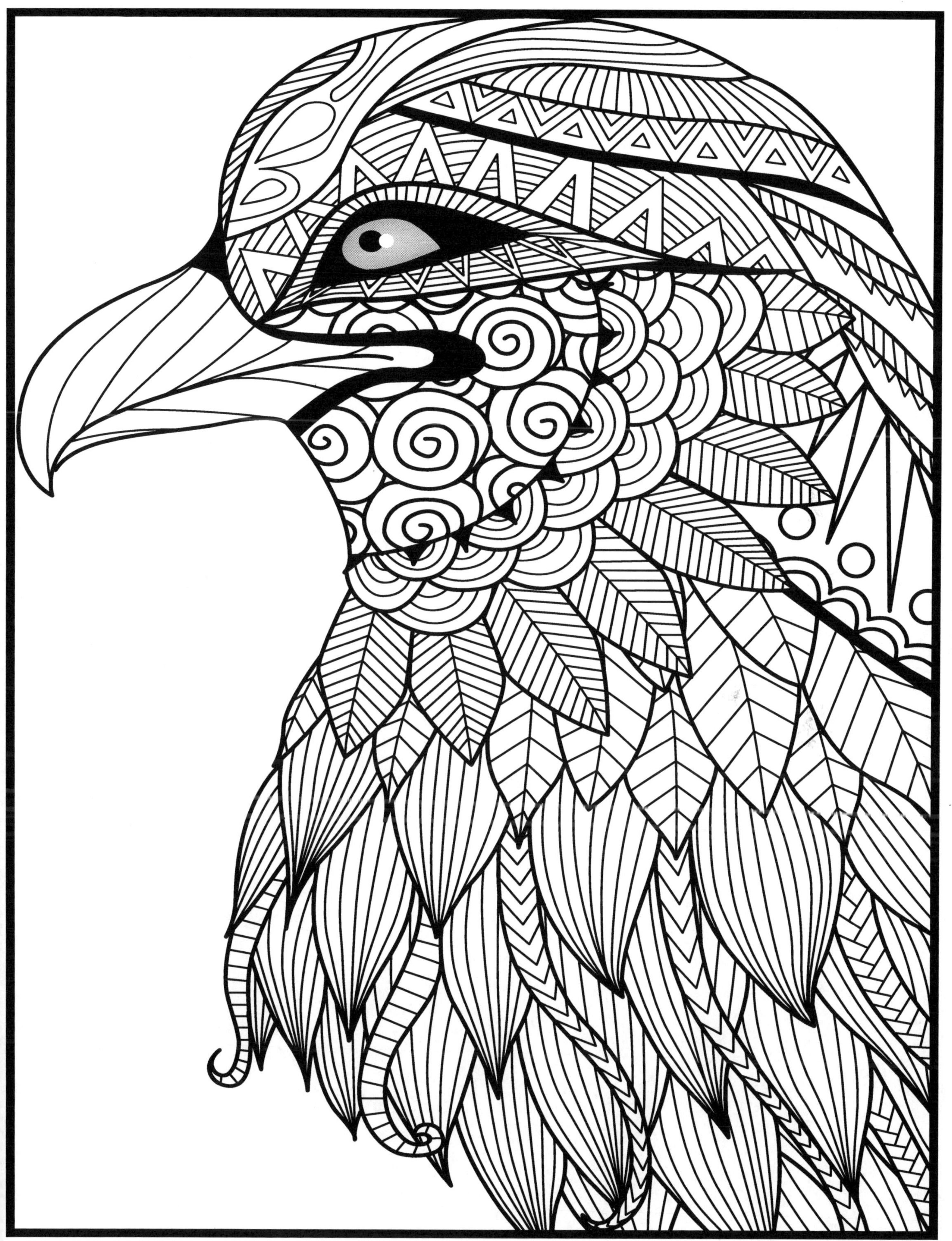

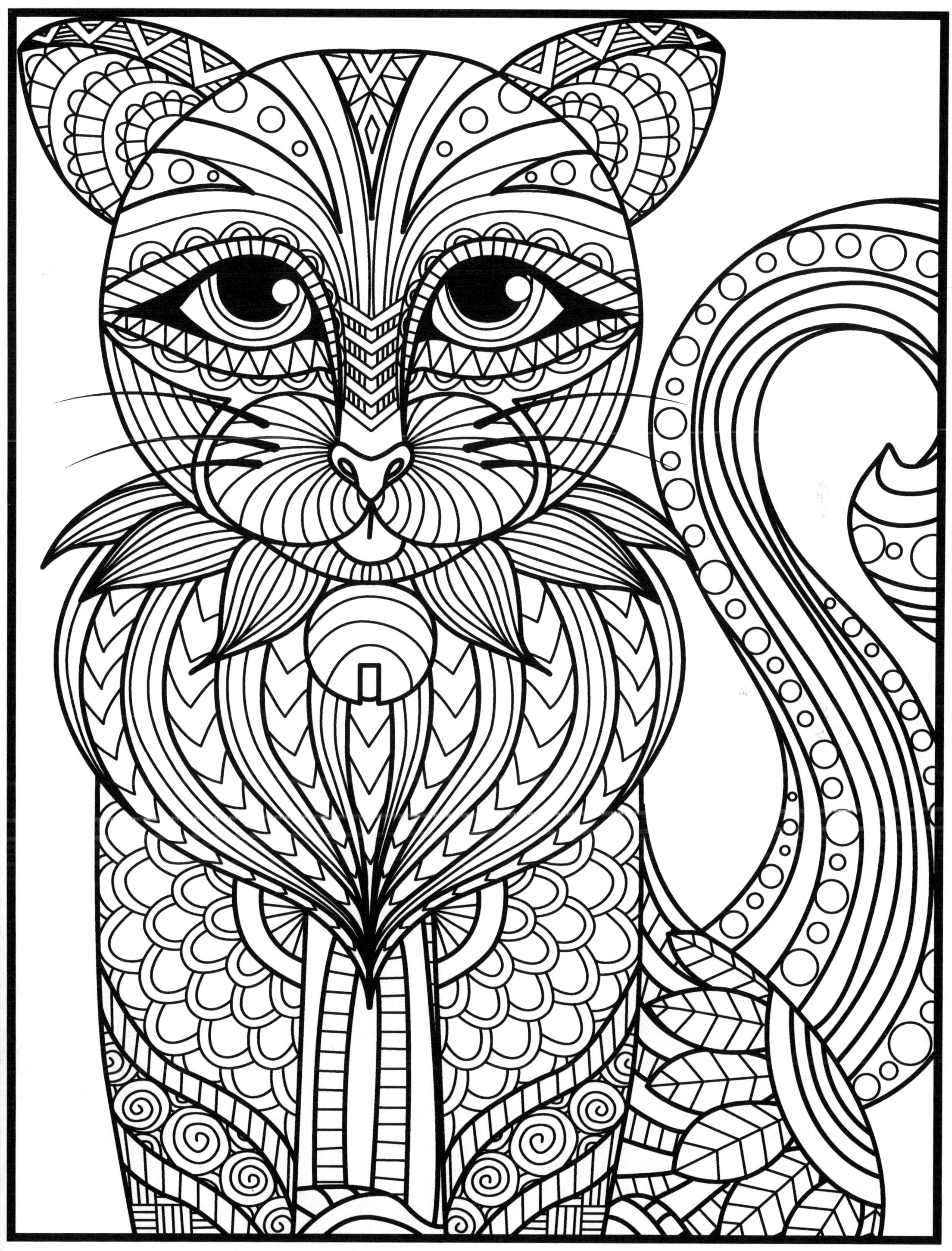

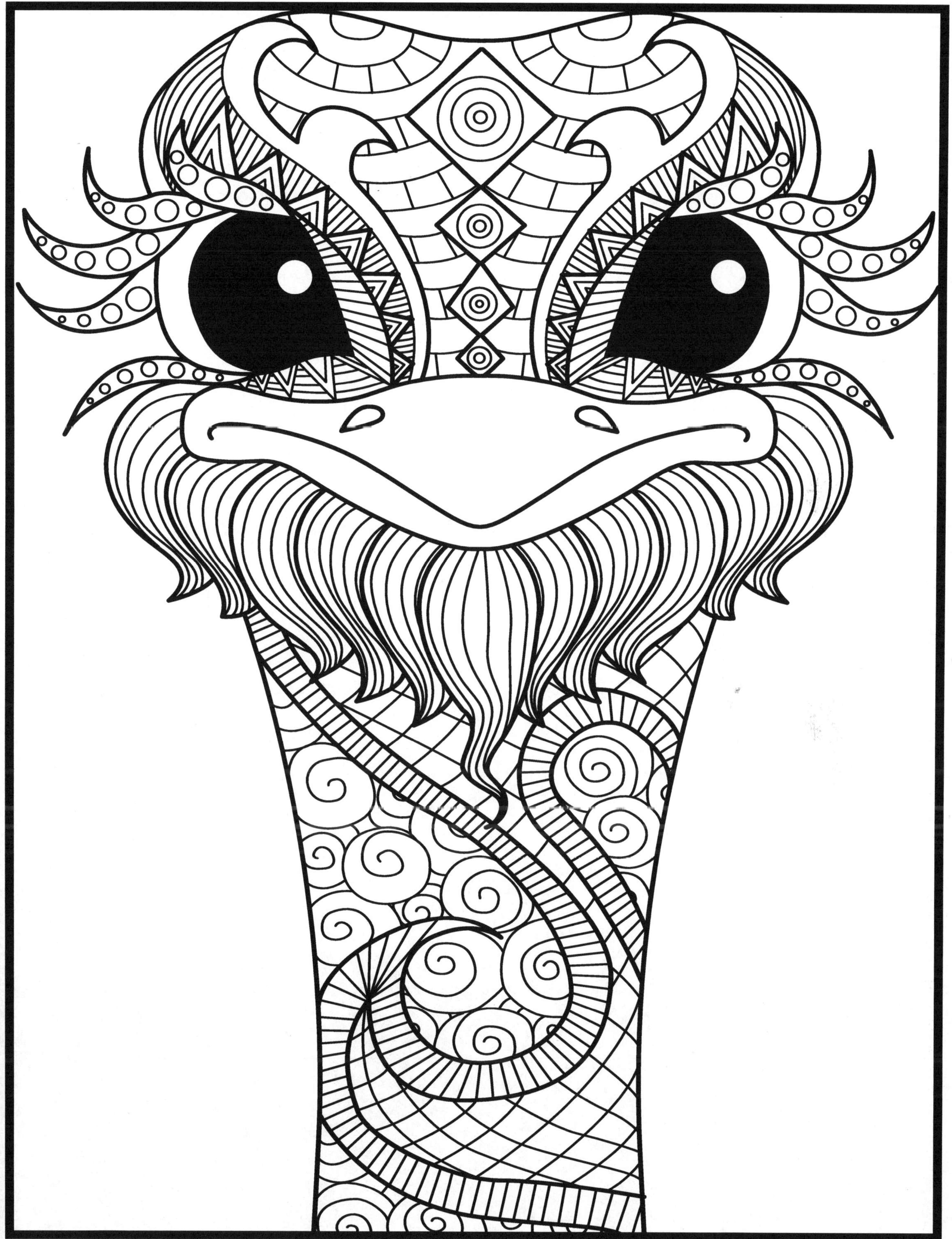

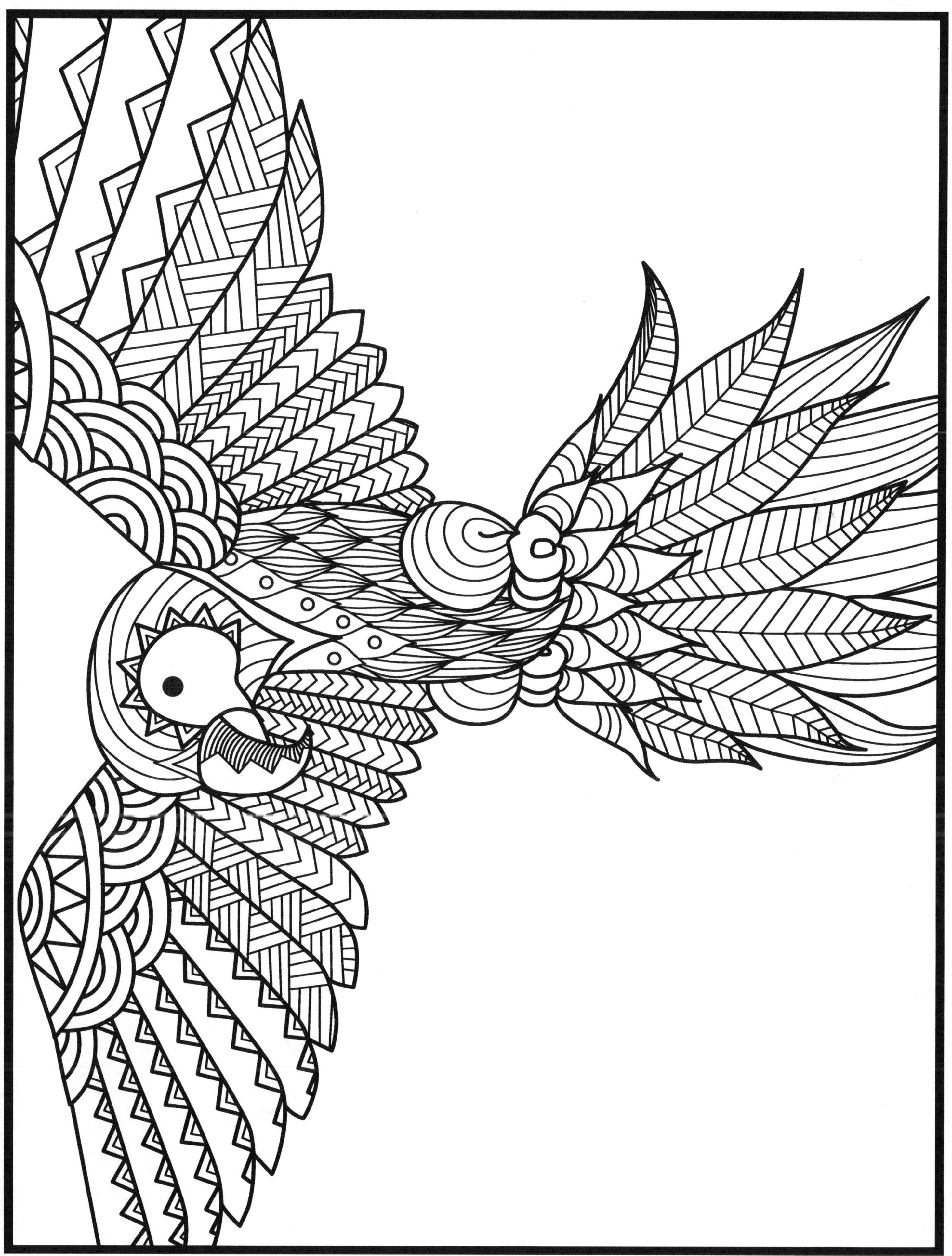

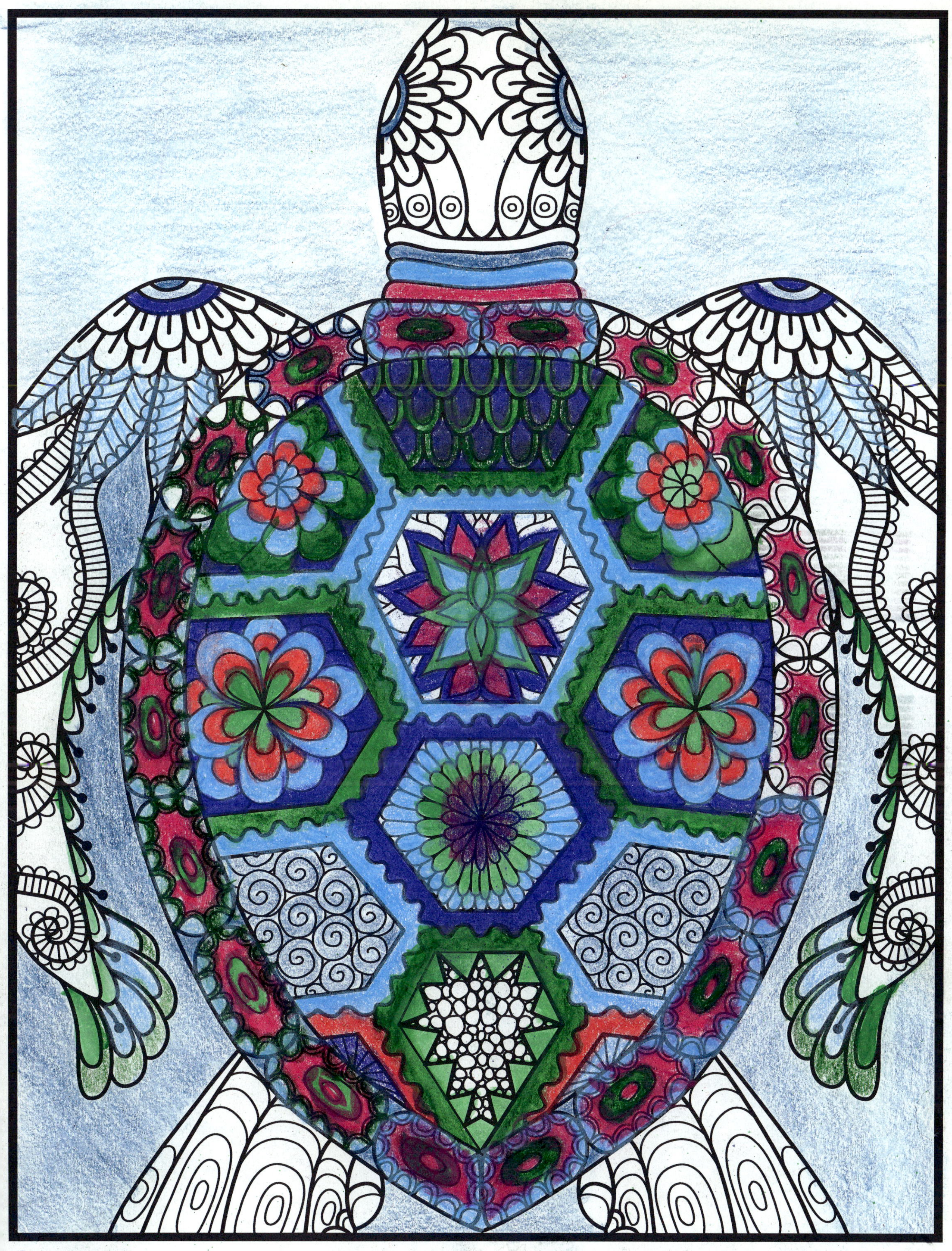

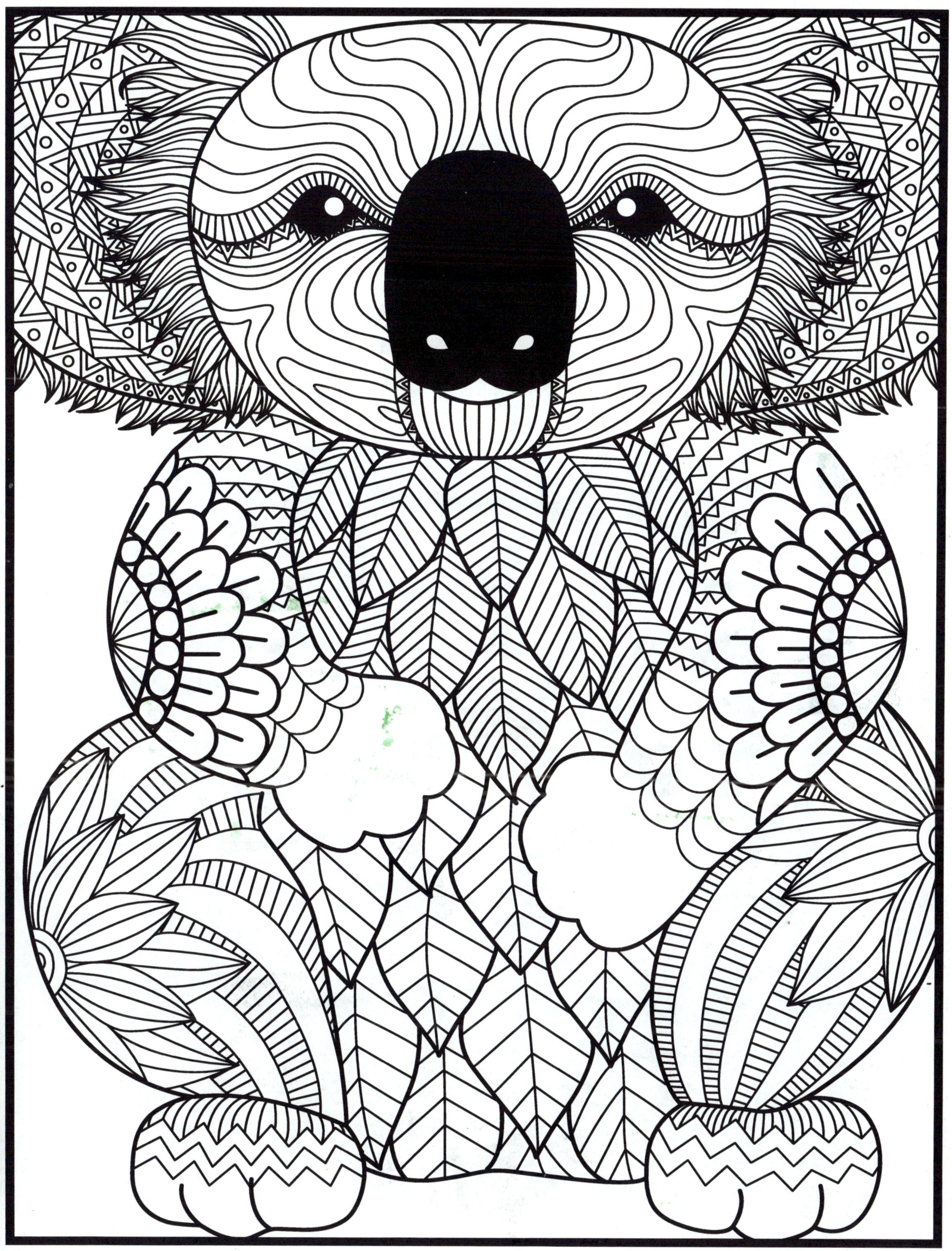

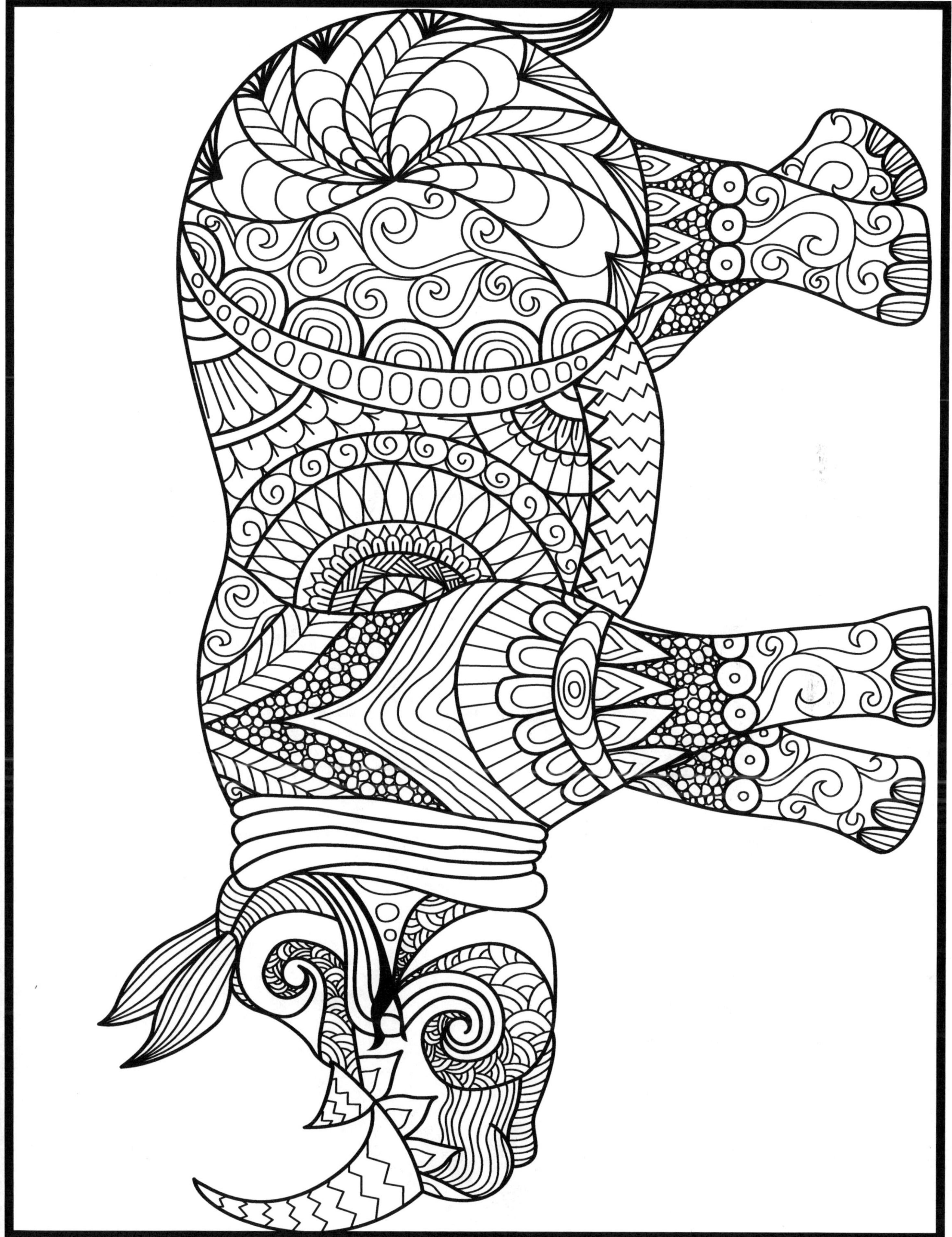

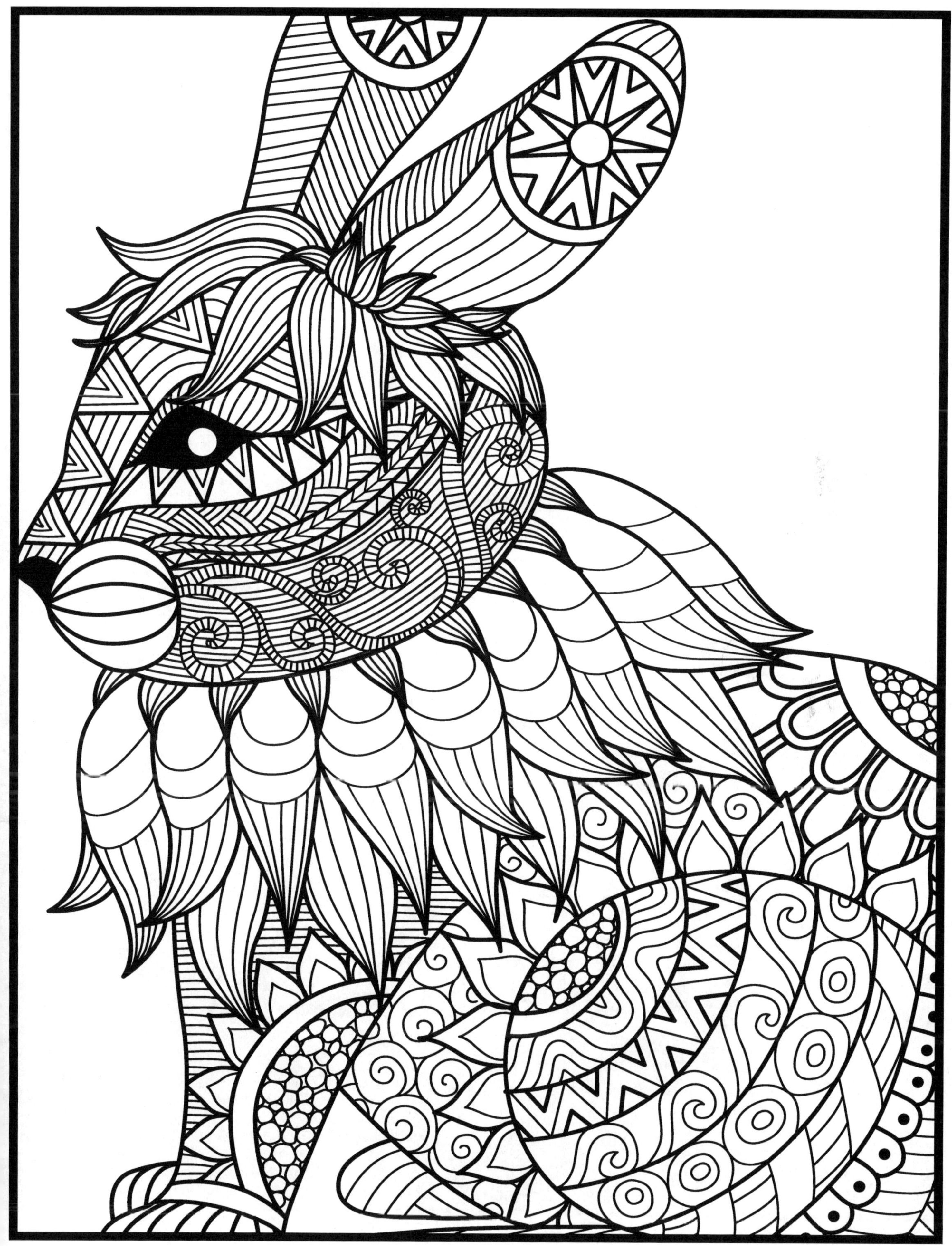

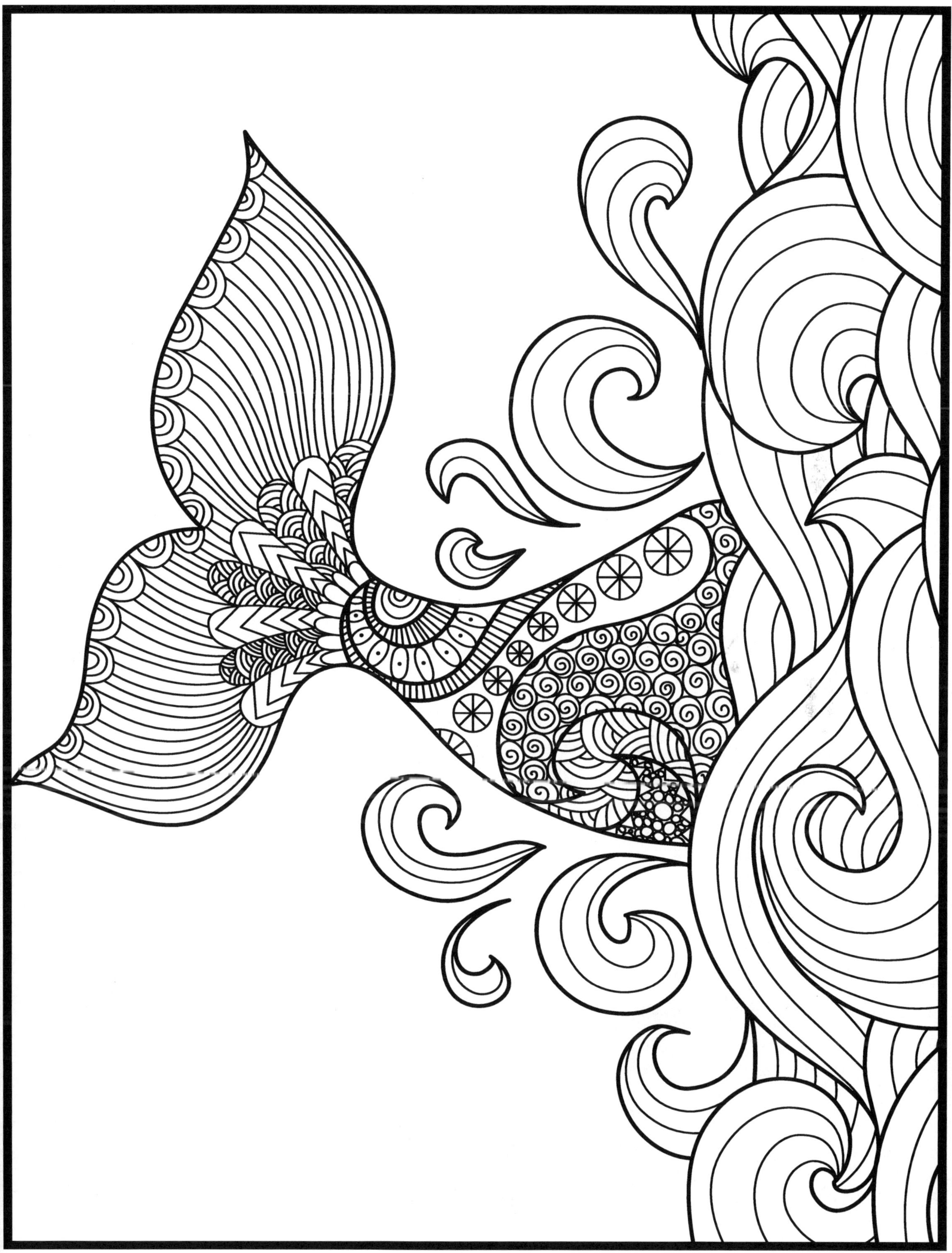

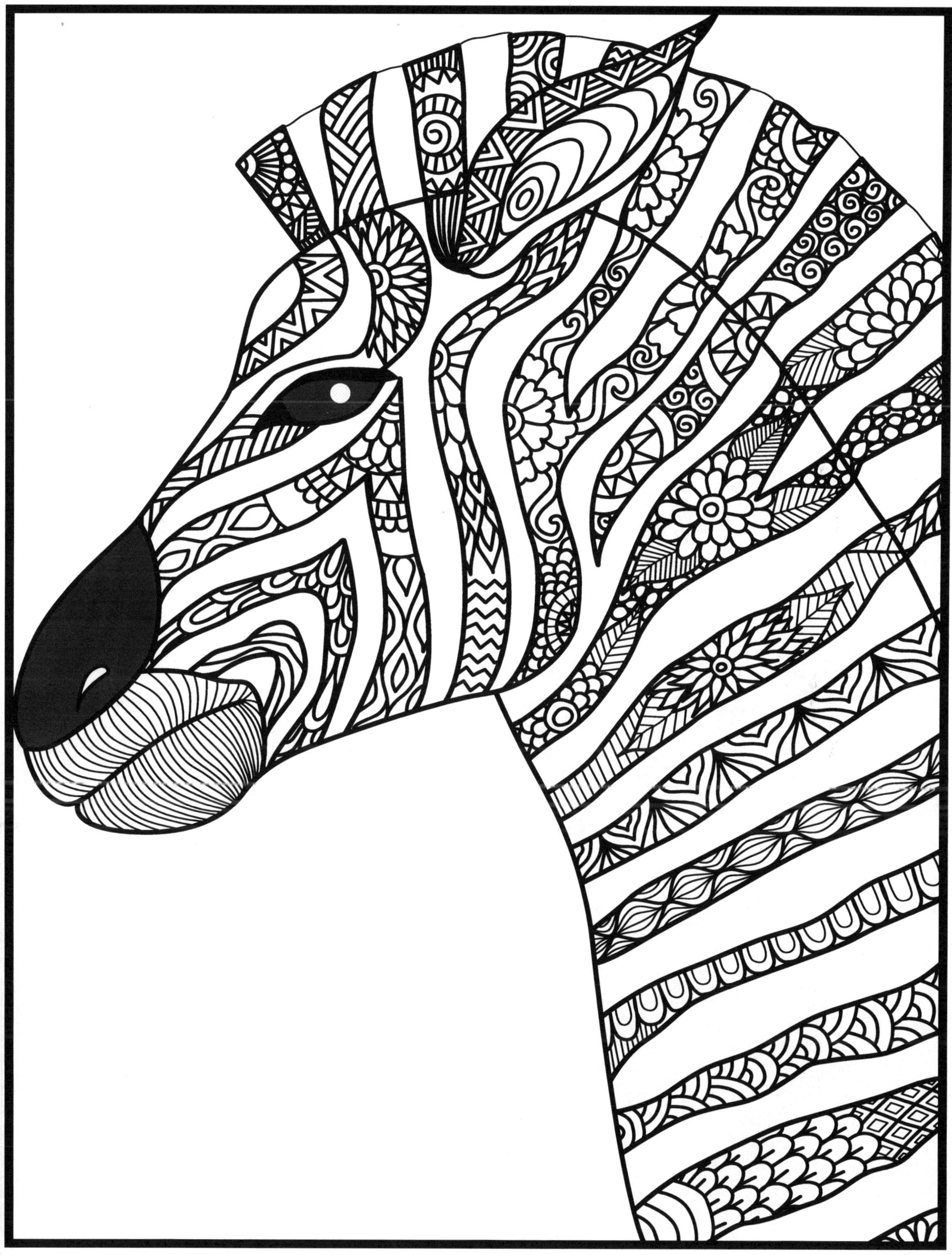

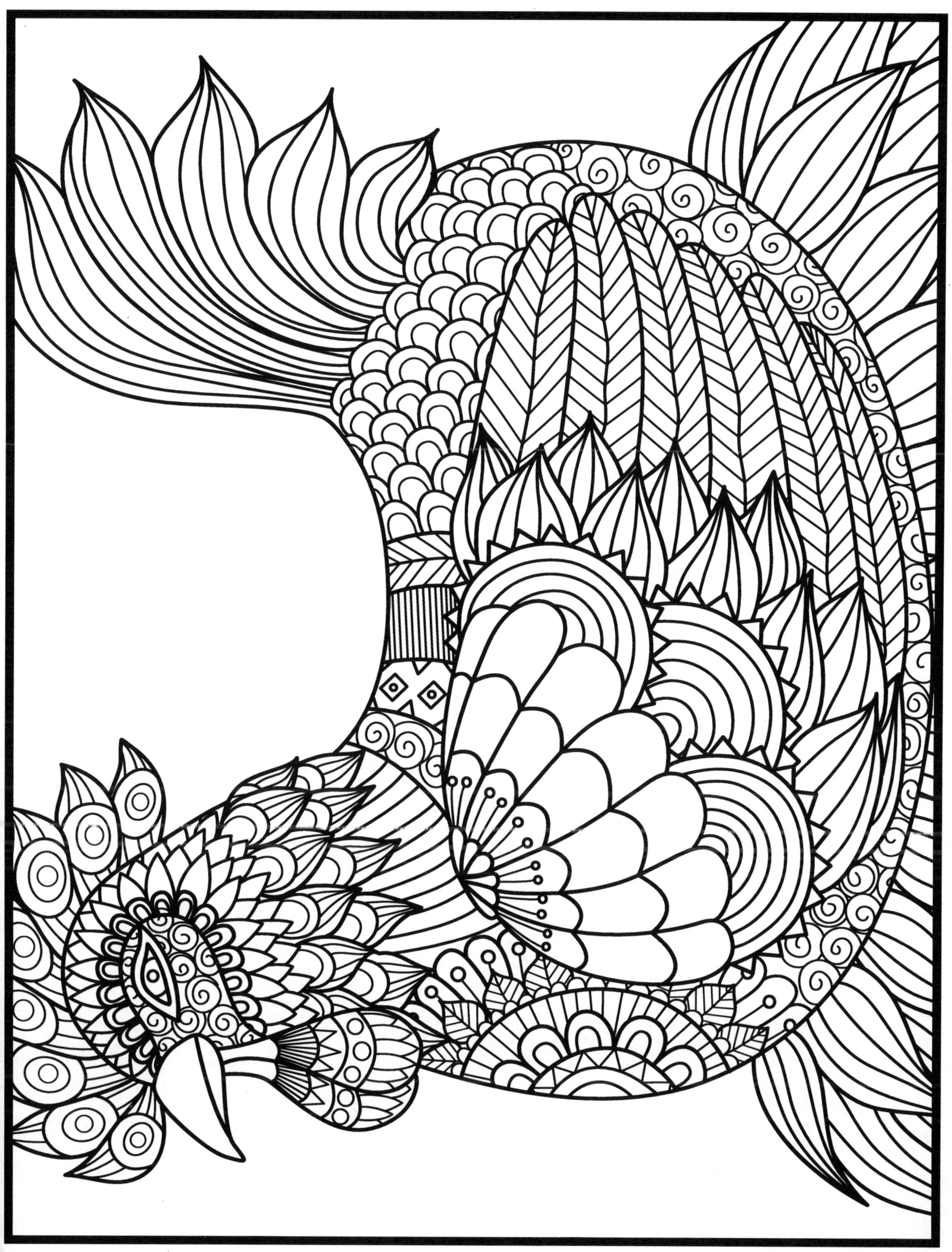

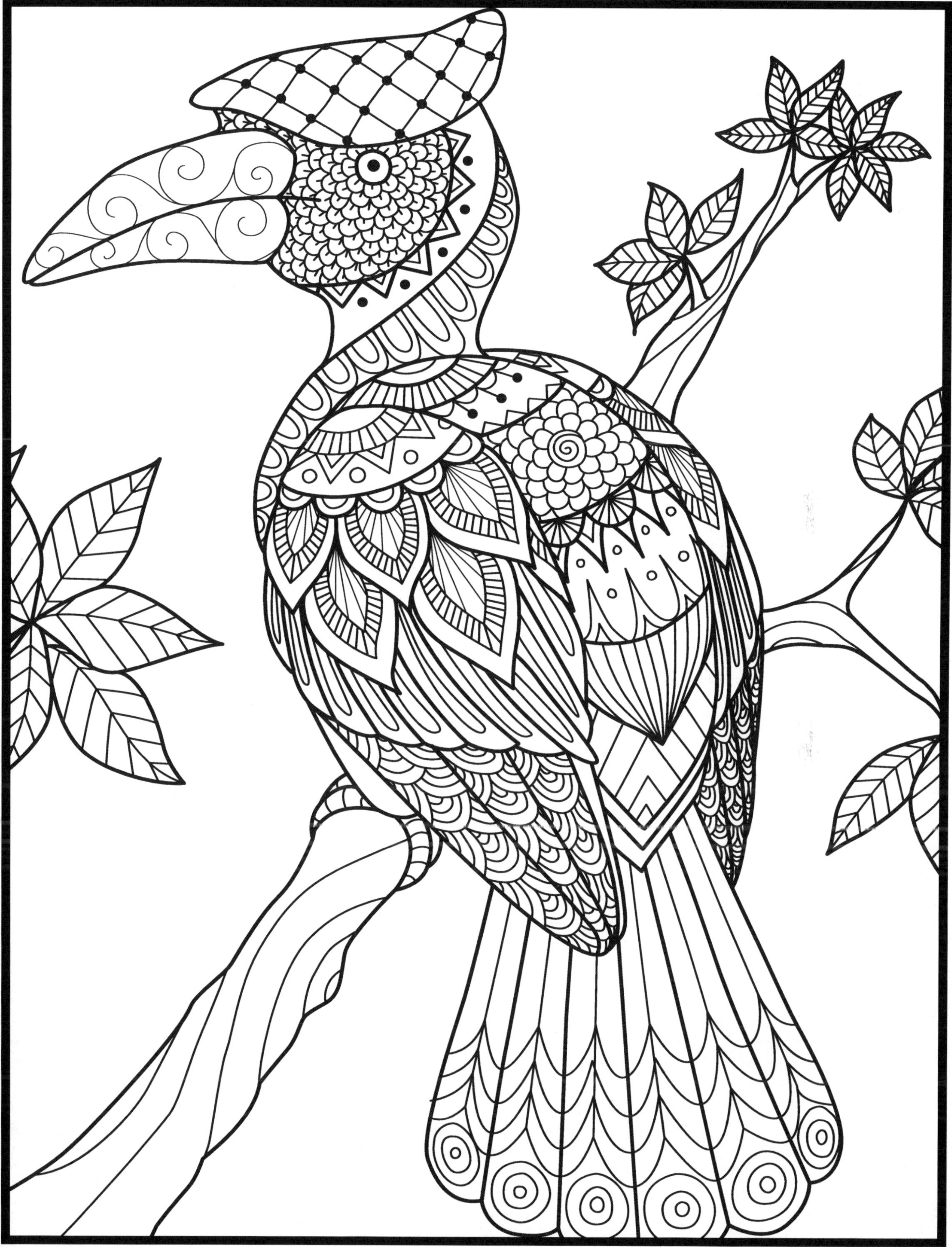

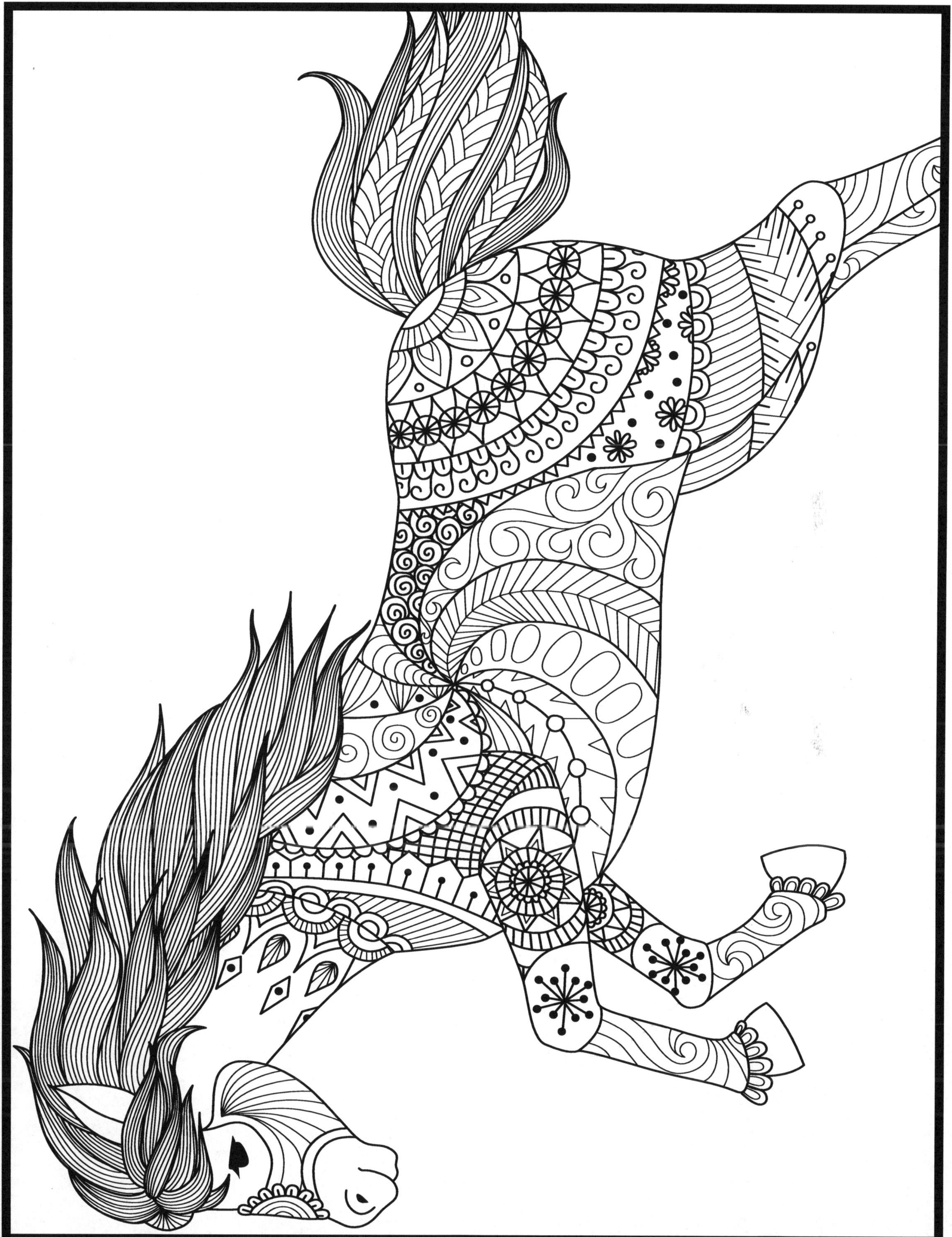

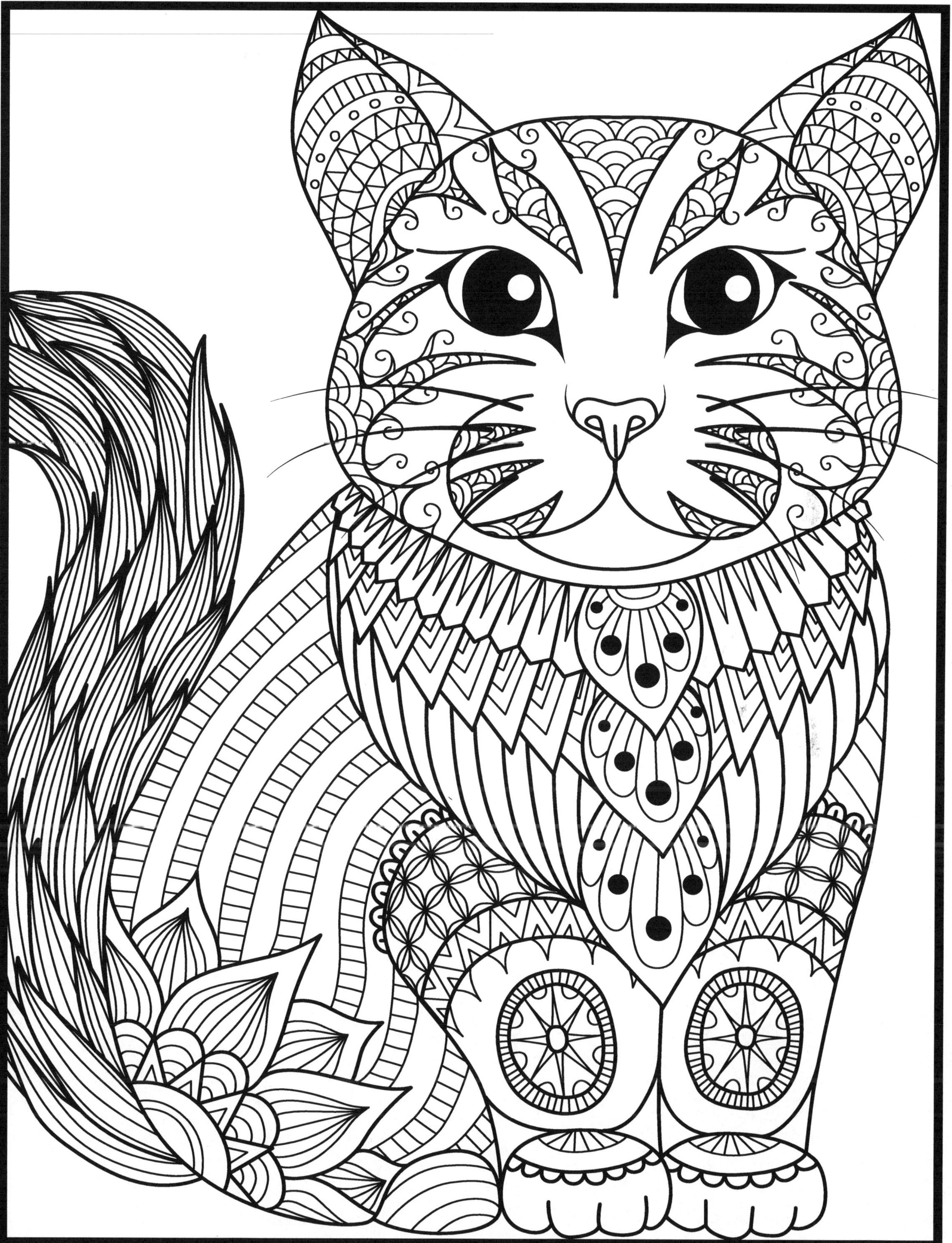

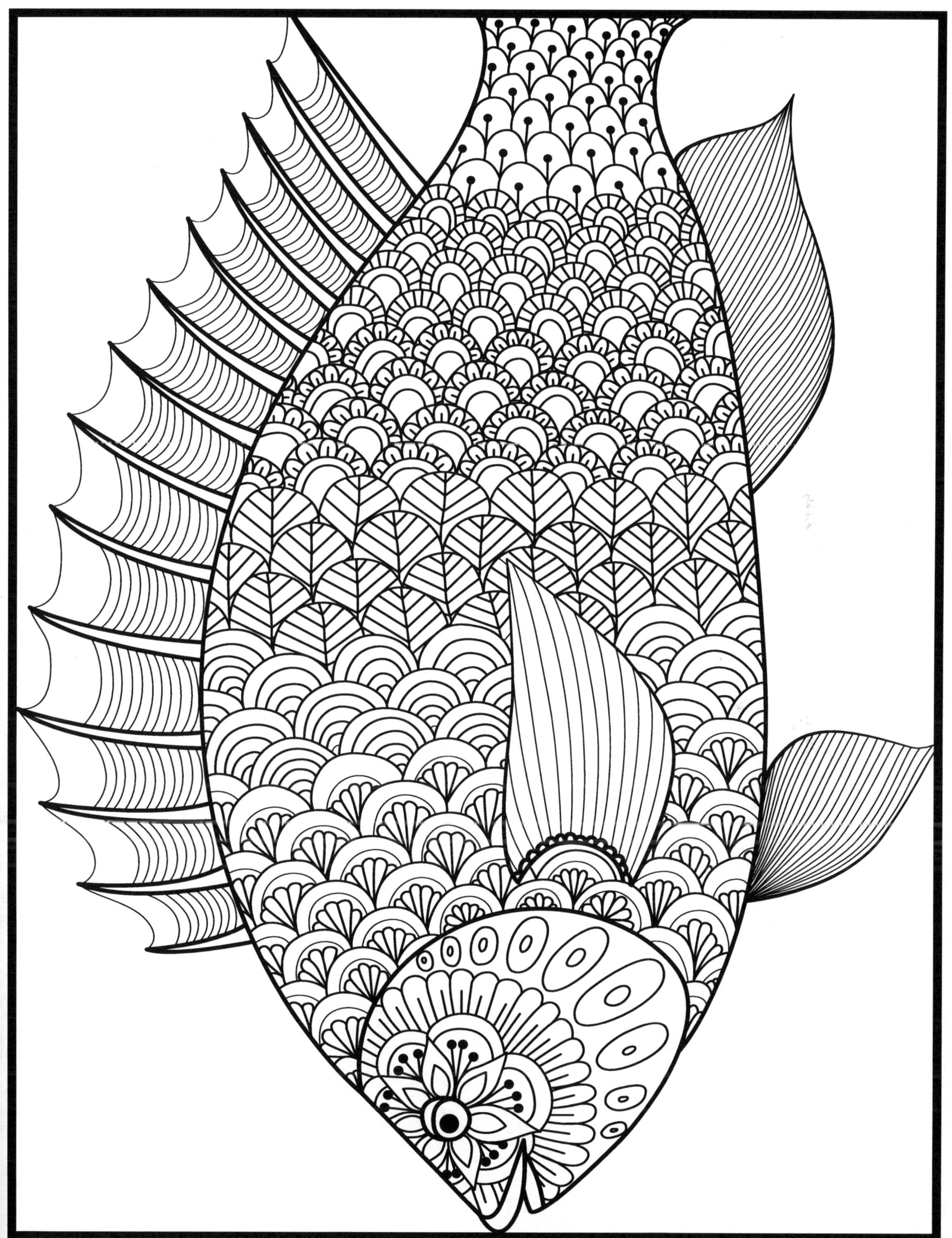

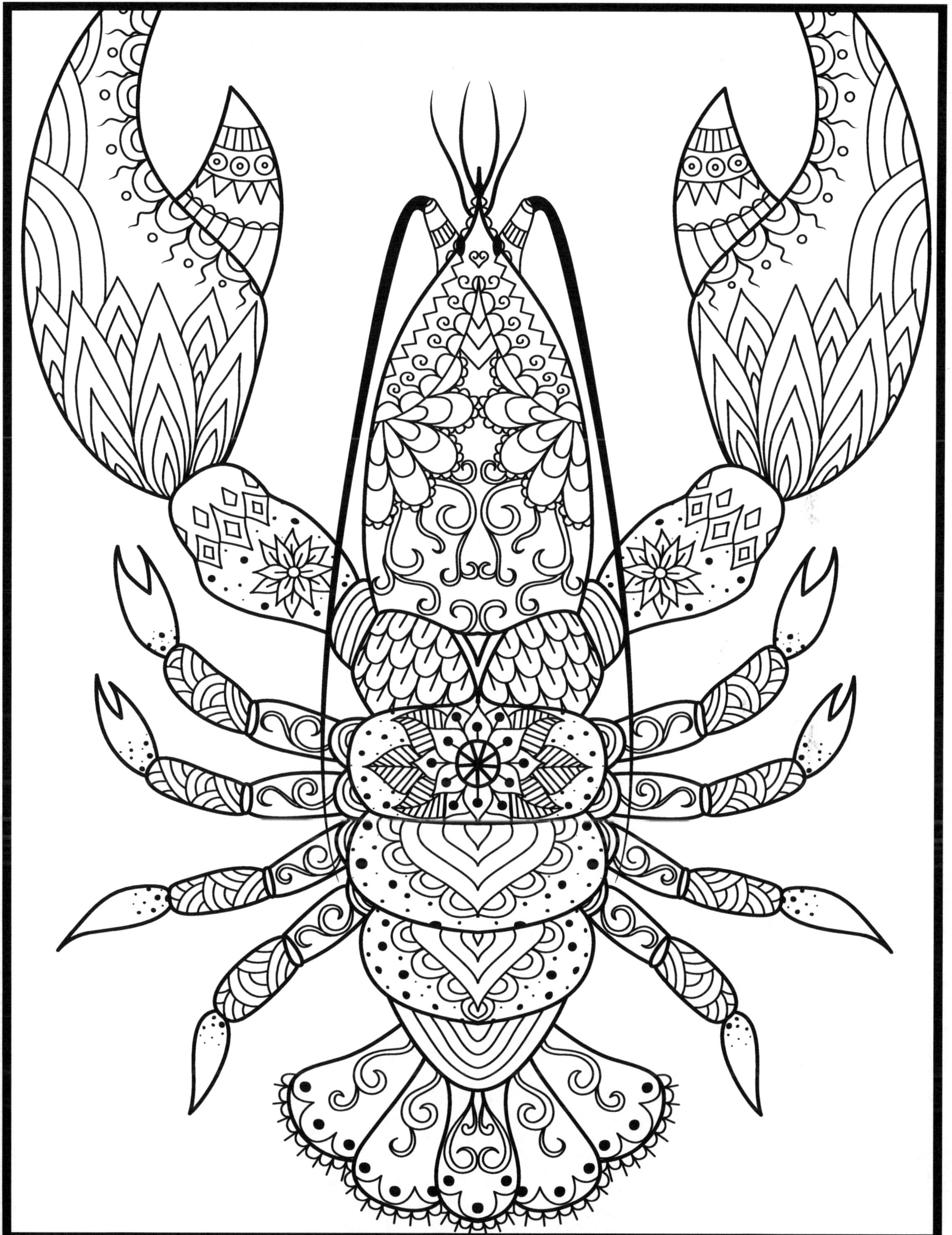

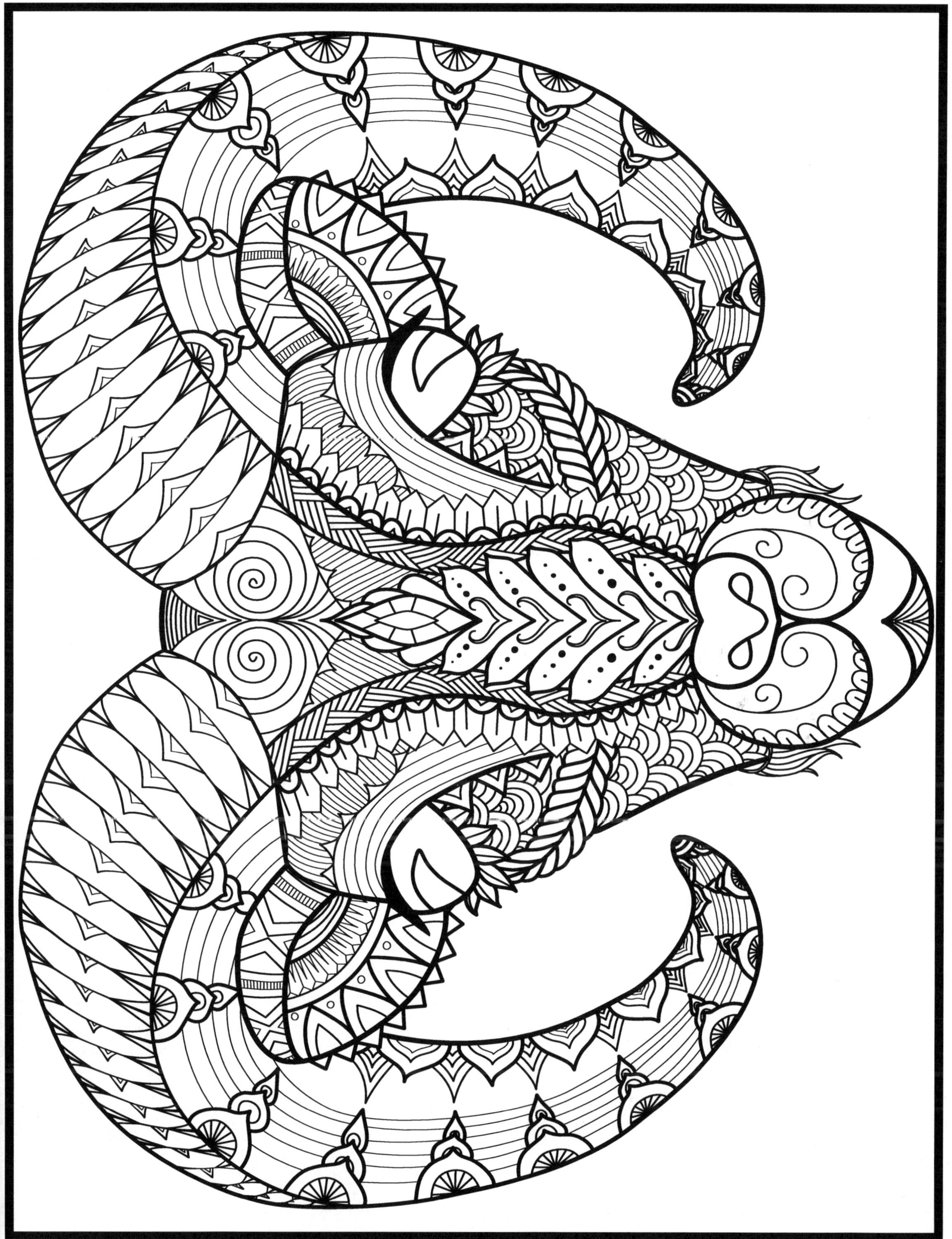

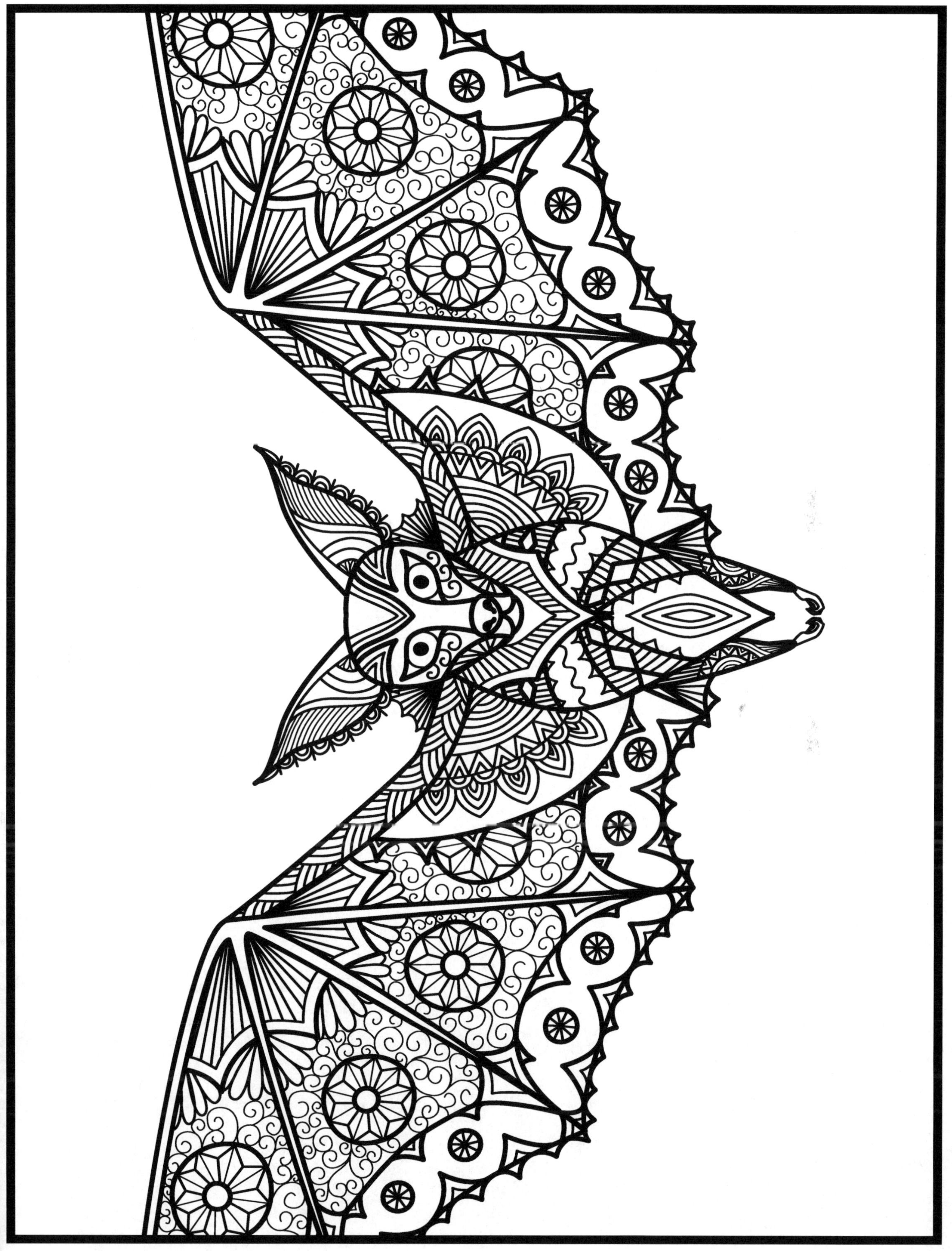

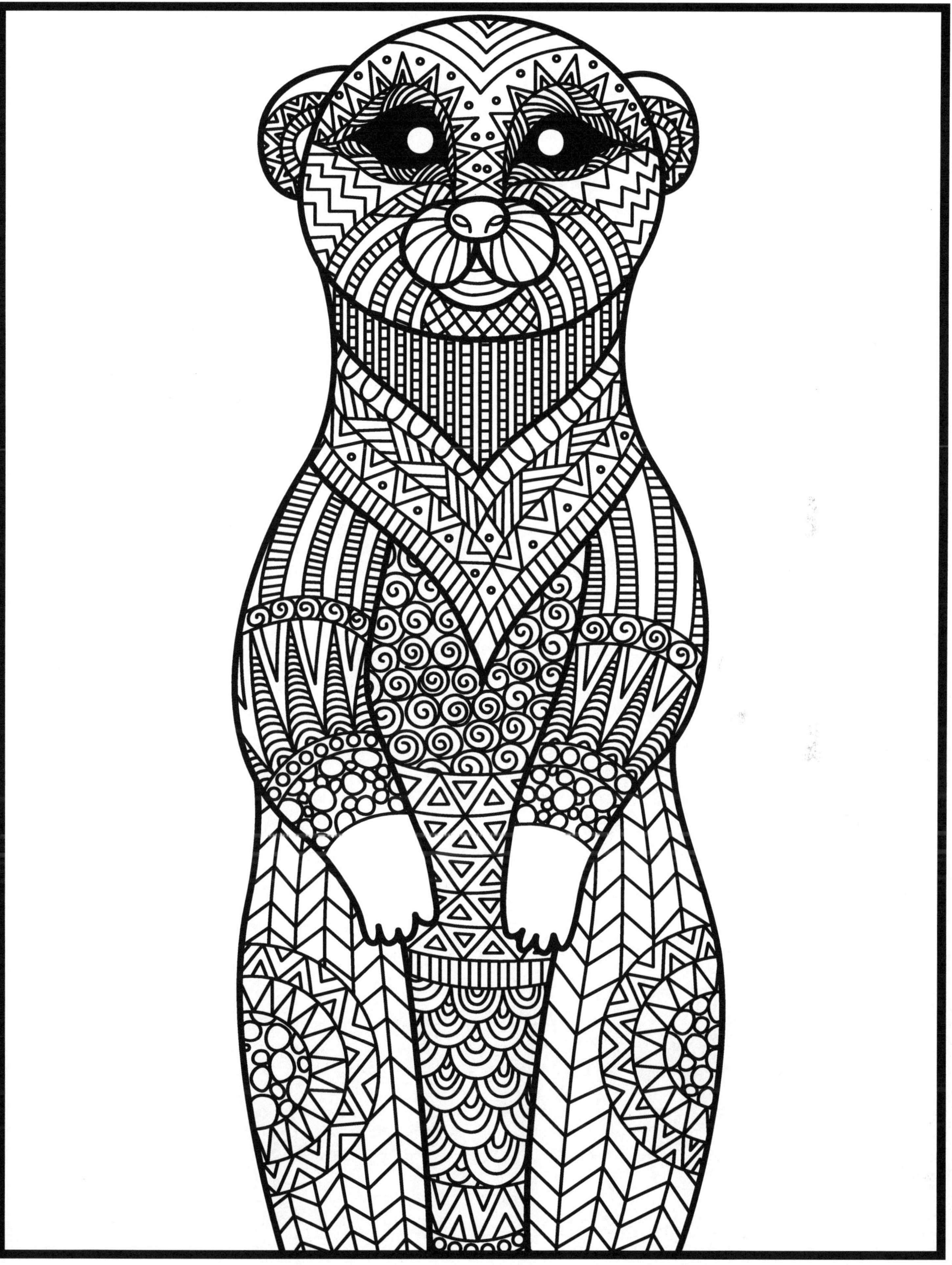

THANK YOU PLEASE LEAVE US A REVIEW ON AMAZON

Made in the USA
San Bernardino, CA
25 July 2016